T0281808

"In the modern world, natio...... ...... as individuals will need to be creative, resourceful and bold when it comes to learning and leadership. Brian Caswell and David Chiem provide a thought-provoking and easy-to-read guide to what is necessary to prosper in an information-rich world."

The Hon Christopher Bowen MP
Australian Shadow Treasurer

"In an age of mass communication that has fuelled an information explosion, there is no doubt that our children need to be encouraged to be bold and creative individuals who develop sound strategies for dealing with the information they encounter in their world. More importantly, we need children to understand that information does not equal knowledge and that neither is the same as wisdom. The strength of *The 3-Mind Revolution* is that it challenges existing notions of what is most important for education. Parents will find this book a helpful counter to narrow consumptive approaches to learning and education."

Professor Trevor Cairney
University of NSW, Sydney

"This book is thought-provoking and challenging, yet accessible and engaging. It will provide support, ideas and ways forward for educators wanting to foster children's multiple intelligences and equip them to be lifelong learners. In this era of increasing globalisation,

i

the authors' strong social justice message, regarding the need to ensure that information technologies unite us in cooperative and productive endeavour is one we should all heed."

Professor Margot Hillel
Australian Catholic University, Melbourne

"Predict, prepare and prevail in a post-Pentium world with this breakthrough analysis of the power of a triune mind."

Mike Denoma
CEO, GLH Hotels Ltd

"Our information age calls for a radical rethink of education. David Chiem and Brian Caswell address this in a compelling, imaginative and original way. *The 3-Mind Revolution* is a timely call to action for parents, leaders and educators alike, as well as an indispensable collection of insights into the mind of a 21st Century Champion."

Professor Allan Snyder FRS
Founder and Director of the Centre for the Mind
150th Chair of Science, University of Sydney

"Delightfully written and persuasively argued, *The 3-Mind Revolution* will undoubtedly stimulate conversation about one of the driving issues of our time – our children's education."

Professor Kathy Hirsh-Pasek
Senior Fellow, Brookings Institution
Co-Author of Einstein Never Used Flashcards

"As an architectural educator the book touches on many issues and concepts that I find very relevant and I am amazed how such complex ideas have been so simply and clearly presented. The book is a must read for all teachers, parents and kids!"

Professor Tay Kheng Soon
Professor, National University of Singapore

The 3-Mind Revolution

A New World View for Global Leaders, Educators and Parents

2nd Edition

DAVID CHIEM & BRIAN CASWELL

 **World Scientific**

W JERSEY · LONDON · SINGAPORE · BEIJING · SHANGHAI · HONG KONG · TAIPEI · CHENNAI · TOKYO

Published by

World Scientific Publishing Co. Pte. Ltd.

5 Toh Tuck Link, Singapore 596224

USA office: 27 Warren Street, Suite 401-402, Hackensack, NJ 07601

UK office: 57 Shelton Street, Covent Garden, London WC2H 9HE

National Library Board, Singapore Cataloguing-in-Publication Data
Name(s): Chiem, David Phu An. | Caswell, Brian, 1954–   author.
Title: The 3-mind revolution : a new world view of global leaders, educators and parents /
    David Chiem & Brian Caswell.
Other titles: Three-mind revolution.
Description: 2nd edition. | Singapore : World Scientific, 2016. |
    First published by Marshall Cavendish Editions in 2009.
Identifier(s): OCN 959918725 | ISBN 978-981-32-0086-9
Subject(s): LCSH: Cognition in children. | Child development. |
    Self-actualization (Psychology) in children.
Classification: DDC 155.413--dc23

British Library Cataloguing-in-Publication Data
A catalogue record for this book is available from the British Library.

Desk Editor: Dong Lixi

Printed in Singapore

With Sincere Thanks:

To Jacqueline Elfick, our tireless honorary editor and friend, without whom our words – and our ideas – would flow less freely.

To Professor Allan Snyder, Professor Kathy Hirsh-Pasek, Professor Roberta Golinkoff, Professor Trevor Cairney, Tay Kheng Soon, Kylie Bell, Sophie Ellwood, Miki Kanamaru, and Carmee Lim for your invaluable comments and suggestions.

To Kim Nguyen, Tina Tan and Christopher Minjoot, for your hard and patient work in bringing it all together.

*

To our parents, whose sacrifices and vision provided us with the 3 Minds long before we knew what they were.

And, as always, to our wives:

Catherine, for grounding my life, so that I take the time to see the stars – David.

and

Marlene, who provides the foundation of love, upon which everything else I do is built – Brian.

Contents

"The medium is the message..."[i]

– Marshall McLuhan
Understanding Media: The Extensions of Man

Foreword

Knowledge, they say, is doubling every two to two-and-a-half years. This means that even an impossibly brilliant scholar who knows every fact today, would only know half of the information available in just a few short years. For millennia, memorization was the currency of education. The monks of the Middle Ages memorized the bible and stood as the religious authority. And even more recently, in the Industrial Age, our schools trained students in the mastery of fact as the road to substance and critical thinking.

But *the times are a-changing*. In our new, fast-paced world of ever-shifting possibilities, the problems you prepare for might not be the ones you encounter. As Brian Caswell and David Chiem suggest, in this new world order, we will be paid not just for what we know, but for what we can *do* with what we know. In the mid-1980s, we shifted from an industrial-based economy to a knowledge-based one. What did not change however was the education system. There is a joke that if Rip van Winkle were to awaken today, the only familiar institution in his brave new world would be the school system.

The call for a 21st Century education is resounding. In 2006, the New Commission on the Skills of the American Workforce wrote, *"If we continue on our current course, and the number of nations outpacing us in the education race continues to grow at its current rate, the American standard of living will steadily fall relative to those nations, rich and poor, that are doing a better job."*

Speaking to a more global audience, scholars like Professor Robert Sternberg, Dean of the Arts and Sciences at Tufts University, noted that we had to teach skills for life, and that successful students must nurture their analytic, practical and creative intelligence. Professor Howard Gardner of Harvard University also encourages a broader view of the minds needed for a challenging world. In a recent book, he describes the disciplined mind, the synthesizing mind, the creating mind, the respectful mind and the ethical mind.

These giants in the fields of science and education are responding in part to the concerns of business leaders, who worry that college graduates today are not equipped for the workplace of tomorrow.

Brian Caswell and David Chiem are adding their unique voice to the chorus of voices for educational revolution. In this accessible framework, informed by years of classroom teaching, creative filmmaking and novel writing, the authors offer a crisp rationale for an educational system that focuses on social, educational, and creative themes. Like those before them, they argue for a shift from mere content in education to a wider focus on how children learn. Caswell and Chiem focus specifically on understanding the creative process and how this valuable information can assist in designing the curriculum – and even the schools – of the future.

In an article for *Time* magazine, on December 10, 2006, writers Claudia Wallis and Sonia Steptoe ask, *"Can our public schools, originally designed to educate workers for agrarian life and industrial-age factories, make the necessary shifts?"* The book you are about to read suggests that we can and must refocus our education, and that this change will enable all children to reach their potential as 21st Century citizens in a globalized world.

Delightfully written and persuasively argued, *The 3-Mind Revolution* will undoubtedly stimulate conversation about one of the driving issues of our time – our children's education.

Kathy Hirsh-Pasek PhD,
(Lefkowitz Professor of Psychology,
Temple University, Philadelphia)
Co-author of *Einstein Never Used Flashcards* and
A Mandate for Playful Learning

Introduction: Why Do We Need a Revolution?

"Battles are won by the side which, firstly, possesses the greatest competitive advantage, and secondly, makes the fewest mistakes, for every battle is won or lost before it is fought."[ii]

– Sun Tzu
The Art of War

Collision-Course

In the late 1970s, Glen Penfield, a geologist doing survey work for an oil company on Mexico's remote Yucatán Peninsula, made a discovery that finally explained a century-old mystery.

Penfield discovered an impact crater well over 180 kilometres wide near the small town of Chicxulub.

An impact crater is the depression created when a piece of space debris smashes at incredibly high speed into the planet's surface.

The debris that caused the Chicxulub Crater hit the Earth 65 million years ago. It was an asteroid fragment at least 10 kilometres in diameter, travelling at over 50,000 kilometres per hour.

The physical consequences of such a celestial collision cannot be underestimated. In fact, the Chicxulub impact is perhaps the most important single event in the history of the planet; changing the future direction of all life on Earth. This one cataclysmic event ended the Age of Reptiles and kick-started the Age of Mammals.

The energy released by the impact was two million times more powerful than the largest nuclear bomb ever detonated.

It caused kilometre-high tsunamis and sent up a cloud of dust and debris so dense that it blocked out the sun for months, plunging the world into a severe and prolonged winter.

When the dust finally settled, the greenhouse gases, such as carbon dioxide, which had been released, caused a rapid acceleration of global warming.

These dramatic climatic extremes of cold and heat led to the extinction of around 70% of all living species, including the most successful land animals ever – the dinosaurs.

For over 140 million years (roughly a hundred times what human beings have so far managed), dinosaurs were the kings of creation. Then, in one brief moment, it was all over. The environment in which they lived and thrived changed dramatically, and they were unable to change with it.

The smaller but more adaptable mammals survived the disaster. They evolved to create their own dynasty – including *homo sapiens*, the only creature in the history of the planet with the ingenuity to intentionally alter its own environment.

And alter our environment we most certainly have.

From the pollution of the Industrial Age to the extinction of thousands of species every year, we are now in danger of leaving behind a world that is un-recognisable and possibly uninhabitable.

We have mortgaged our children's future in the name of progress, and it will take a good deal of ingenuity and imagination on their part to fix all the problems that we have created.

Ingenuity and imagination have always been human-kind's aces in the evolutionary poker game. But will these characteristics remain our most valuable assets, or are they destined to become our curse?

You see, there is another problem emerging, that is, in its own way, just as pressing as the destruction of our environment. Having entered the Information Age, we are now facing a cultural, social and educational crisis which is rapidly changing the world as we know it.

We call this crisis '**The Post-Pentium Apocalypse**'.

Apocalypse?

Contrary to popular belief, the word 'apocalypse' does not mean war, devastation and the end of everything. In Greek, *apokálipsis* means a 'lifting of the veil' or a 'revelation'. So what is this revelation?

The biblical apocalypse describes a dramatic change in Man's relationship with God. The Post-Pentium Apocalypse refers to a dramatic change in our relationship with Information.

Will we find ourselves in a virtual New Jerusalem consisting of greater communication, creativity and freedom, or will we be trampled under the hooves of the Four Horsemen of the Post-Pentium Apocalypse – **Impotence, Ignorance, Inequality and Instability?**

It all depends on how well we, and more importantly, our children, cope with this new wave of change.

But surely things aren't so bad. After all, many of us earn a reasonable living. And aren't we able to enjoy all the fruits of modern life, such as lightning-fast internet, social networking and instant downloads? Doesn't the reach of the world-wide web promise to democratise information, giving us all, for the first time in history, free and equal access to a whole world of knowledge?

Ideally, yes...

But let's stop for a moment and imagine a global environment in which information is available to everyone, but the actual power to produce and control that information is concentrated in the hands of a small number of super-rich individuals – who also own and control the search engines, social media, e-commerce and news-sources through which we access it.

Numerous times in the 20th Century, and now into the 21st, we have seen what can happen when a political regime or a powerful, self-interested individual manages to take effective control of the mass media. Balanced commentary and discussion is pushed to the sidelines, or crushed.

And contrary to its democratic promise, the online world is by no means immune to such manipulation. Look at the effectiveness of ISIS and other fundamentalist groups and their strategy of manipulating the social media to proselytise and radicalise the young and the disaffected.

In fact, rather than universally empowering the individual, the growth of social media platforms and e-commerce have actually created a mechanism for far more personal and individual manipulation, as well as cyber-bullying and trolling – which is why some have dubbed it the '*anti*-social network'.

This is just the thin edge of a dangerous and very far-reaching wedge that could, without a vigilant and educated population, usher in a world where the dissemination of information only reflects the narrow self-interests of a select few: an environment, in which big business and government have access to our every communication, our every thought – where we have ceded our privacy and exposed our most personal secrets in return for the addictive lure of the 'social' media and the vague, undefined promise of 'security' in an insecure world. A world where the siren call of 'personal' connection can be hijacked by business to 'micro-target' their advertising, or by fundamentalists, extremists and predators to radicalise and victimise the young.

In such a world, the universal reach of the internet, rather than being a force for democracy and equality, might easily allow unscrupulous politicians, powerful individuals, or fanatically-motivated and determined splinter-groups to alter the truth to suit their own agenda and carry large swathes of the unprepared in the population along with them.

Is it so hard to imagine:

- a world governed by a new incarnation of feudalism, where poverty and unemployment co-exist with wealth and privilege?

- a world where education has failed the majority of children and the enormous democratic and creative potential of the Information Age remains unrealised?

- a world where our inherent drive to belong has been subverted by the faceless agendas of opportunists and fanatics.

Looking around us, unfortunately, it is not.

Such a world becomes a possibility if people lose the ability to ask the important questions.

It becomes inevitable if the general public gradually loses its capacity to evaluate information and engage with it critically.

Technology specialists, social scientists, educators, political observers, business analysts, religious leaders and economists have all warned us that we need to act quickly in the face of rapid change – but what, exactly, can we do?

The first step towards solving any problem is to understand its causes.

So, in order to understand the enormous challenges and opportunities created by the Information Age, let's look first at what has changed in the way we relate to information.

Diamond Rain

Imagine this.

Tomorrow, when you wake up, you swing your legs out of bed, find your slippers with your feet, and make your way across to the window to open the blind and let in the new day.

It is raining. Again.

Nothing particularly unusual, you might think – except that, as you watch the rain falling down outside the window, you realise that this time it is different.

Because, this time, instead of raining... rain, it is raining diamonds. Beautiful, brilliant-cut, high-quality stones – some the size of pigeon eggs, some barely a carat, but all of them perfect.

The breakfast announcer on the radio, his voice even more hysterical than usual, informs you that this miraculous 'diamond rain' phenomenon is repeating itself across the entire planet, on every continent, in every major population centre. Billions and billions of the precious stones, falling like a gift from the heavens.

For a moment, it is better than Christmas. A fortune dropping out of the sky; yours to pick up and possess.

You rush outside to fill your pockets. Perhaps you take a shopping bag, so that you can gather even more of the treasure.

Some of your neighbours are already out there, raking the stones into piles, shovelling them into wheel-barrows or sacks, smiling like Aladdin in the cave of the forty thieves.

But then you stop, as the realisation strikes.

There is no point in rushing to gather up the gems, to store them away like a squirrel's cache of winter nuts.

The phenomenon is worldwide. Which means...

That from today on, diamonds will be as common, worldwide, as pebbles or rocks.

That the value of a diamond will, therefore, be about the same as that of a pebble or a rock.

Virtually worthless.

Unfortunately, that hard reality also applies to the diamonds which, in the past, you spent so much of your hard-earned salary to buy...

We live, today, in an era akin to the diamond rain of this imaginary scenario. The sky has not unleashed a storm of the once-precious stones, of course, but human ingenuity has (almost overnight) devalued what has been, for most of human history, the most valuable commodity known to Man – information.

Like the diamonds in our story, it falls from the air around us, bidding us to pick it up and use it, but – as we will discover later – its very availability renders it, in and of itself, almost valueless.

In the world of the Information Revolution, our concepts of information and knowledge – and of education itself – are in drastic need of a rethink.

Information, Knowledge and Wisdom

In an interview given in 1983, scientist and author Arthur C. Clarke made this important observation:

> *"Information – in the sense of raw data – is not knowledge, knowledge is not wisdom, and wisdom is not foresight. Each grows out of the other and we need them all."*[iii]

A far more ancient saying states: *"Abundance of knowledge does not teach men to be wise."*[iv]

That was Heraclitus, who lived about 2,500 years ago. When he uttered those prophetic words, the distinction between knowledge and information was not as stark as it is now.

The past few decades have seen an explosion in the sum – and the availability – of information worldwide, but as Clarke points out, there is a vast difference between information and knowledge.

Today, the first step to wisdom is to draw a distinction between the two.

Information is raw data; facts and figures about anything and everything in the Universe. It surrounds us. It swamps us. It clogs the portals of cyberspace and threatens to bury us in a digital avalanche.

Where information differs from knowledge, is in our **understanding**. It is our ability to make sense of information, and to make use of it creatively and effectively, that transforms it from mere information to true knowledge.

Wisdom is the ability to draw upon our understanding – through our past experiences – to predict the results of decisions and act to produce the best outcomes.

As we will demonstrate in the following pages, the explosion of information has not been matched by an explosion of knowledge or wisdom. This book has been written to address this gap.

A Revolution of the Mind...

Alvin Toffler, the 20th Century's most famous futurist, once wrote:

> 'The illiterate of the twenty-first Century will not be those who cannot read and write,

but those who cannot learn, unlearn and relearn.'[v]

In 1990, when it was written, this kind of thinking was considered revolutionary. Unfortunately, over a quarter of a century later, for many, it still is.

With this in mind, we intend, in this book, to propose a blueprint for a new revolution.

It is not a book heavy with theory and background, dripping with detail and replete with research – all that you can read in our other books[vi].

Rather, it is a poem to progress; a call to action – a brief study of the near future and the demands it will make upon each of us. And of the tools we must develop to meet those demands.

As we journey towards a future very different from the one imagined even by our parents, it is important to understand where we are – and where we have come from. For this reason, we begin the journey by briefly looking back at the landscape of our past.

The present has its roots in that past landscape, just as the future has its own in what we do right now, and though the same Heraclitus rightly advises that *'you cannot step twice into the same river,'*[vii] the lessons that we can learn by retracing its flow will help us to understand how we have come to this crucial fork, and why we need to choose the faster flowing of the streams ahead.

Throughout the book, we use the word 'revolution' very deliberately – because, unlike 'evolution', which implies a passive and gradual response, revolution implies action and positive intent.

Because, in a world created by the exponential growth of digital technology, it is, quite simply, too late for a gradual evolution.

The dinosaurs became extinct, precisely because the rapid changes which swept over their world all those millions of years ago provided them with no opportunity to evolve – to gradually adapt to the new environment.

Thankfully, we are not dinosaurs – though some of our institutions might well be described that way.

We are creative, adaptive, intelligent creatures, with the innate capacity to respond to change – and meet it with innovation.

But in order to innovate – in order to respond with the creative mindset which faces challenges head-on and solves them – we must accept that a new world demands a new way of thinking. And that a new way of thinking demands a better way of preparing the mind.

In a world as fragile as ours, the competitive ethic of the Industrial Age is out-dated and dangerously counter-productive.

If we are to survive and thrive in the face of global warming, population pressures, famine, war, fundamentalism, universal mistrust and periodic economic meltdowns, we will need to mature as a species. We will need to learn to work in cooperation, rather than competition; to seek out the strengths in ourselves, and in others, and celebrate them – instead of searching for weaknesses to excuse or exploit.

And we must look at knowledge not as a reservoir of facts to store and recall, but as raw material to assimilate, synthesise and transform to produce innovations and solutions.

In a changing world, we need to be emotionally balanced, information savvy and, above all, creative.

The Champion Mind. The Learning Mind. The Creative Mind. This is the Trinity of Human Talents; the Three Minds that make One.

In a simpler world, to educate one aspect of Mind may well have been enough, but the world is no longer simple.

The 3-Mind Revolution is our way of dealing with that inescapable fact.

Be Prepared

"For every battle is won or lost before it is fought..." These words are part of the epigraph that began this introduction. Sun Tzu wrote them almost two and a half thousand years ago.

His message was simple: That we must prepare by predicting challenges and developing solutions, **before we are caught up in the battle itself**. That way, we avoid repeating the mistakes of the past, and give ourselves the strategic advantage.

You don't wait until someone is drowning to teach her to swim.

We stand today, on the verge of a brave new world, in an era rich with exciting possibilities – if only we can look forward with a clear vision, and learn from the mistakes of the past.

*

The history of humankind has been, for the most part, one of slow, torturous evolution – with occasional (and famous!) explosions of insight and invention.

The high points, which history so rightly celebrates include:

i)   The wisdom of Confucius and Lao Tze in China in the 4th and 5th Centuries BCE;

ii)   the Golden Age of Athens from Socrates to Plato and Aristotle in the 4th and 5th Centuries BCE and their philosophical successors during the height of the Roman Empire.

iii)   the scientific and mathematical insights born in Ancient Persia and India during the 4th and 5th Centuries BCE, and the innovations of later Islamic mathematicians;

iv) the dedication of medieval scholars and religious orders, who kept the flame of learning alive, and tended the embers of literacy in Europe throughout the Dark Ages;

v) the scholarship of the Byzantine Empire, which gave birth, indirectly, to the Renaissance world of Da Vinci and Michelangelo in the 15th Century;

vi) Gutenberg's development, in 1439, of the printing press – arguably the most important and world changing invention of the last 2000 years;[viii]

vii) the flowering of scientists and artists and
philosophers, including René Descartes and Sir
Isaac Newton, during the Age of Reason in the
18th Century AD.

and, of course,

viii) the amazing theoretical and technological developments of the 19th and 20th Centuries, as symbolised by Thomas Edison and Albert Einstein

These bright, brief moments in the story are spectacular and dazzling, blinding us to the long centuries where progress and enlightenment were far less brilliant!

So, why talk now of revolution? If the history of Man is a history of slow, uneven evolution, why write this small book about the need for huge changes?

For the answer to this question, take a look at the following graph.

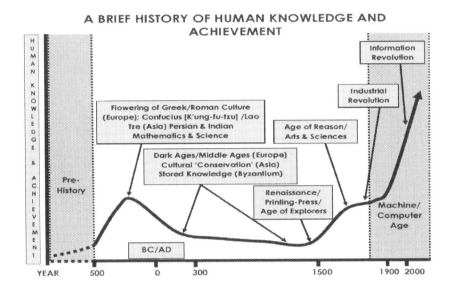

The Industrial Revolution began in 1710, when Newcomen invented his first steam engine, and a steady stream of technological innovations followed. We left behind the world of physical labour and plunged headlong into a bewildering era of industrialisation, growth and social transformation.

We now find ourselves in the world of the Information Revolution – a world characterized by rapid change, fuzzy boundaries, and no hard and fast rules.

There will be no easy answers for our children. New times demand new strategies.

If our children are to live and thrive in the world of tomorrow, **WE must become the next revolution**.

Chapter 1

The Two Revolutions: How the World Was Changed Forever

Commenting on the potential for the future evolution of the automobile, the *Scientific American* magazine declared:

> *That the automobile has practically reached the limit of its development is suggested by the fact that during the past year no improvements of a radical nature have been introduced.*

That year was 1909!

The automobile is still being steadily improved on and has, for decades, been a powerful and enduring symbol of the Industrial Age.

Today, we live in a world created by two overlapping revolutions.

The first is famous – we learned about it way back in school, if we weren't too busy day-dreaming in the back row.

The second is upon us now, and its effects are so ubiquitous that it is already becoming difficult for a large segment of the world's population to remember – or imagine – a world without its all-pervasive presence.

For many, this latest revolution does not seem like a revolution at all. It arrived without the disruptive social upheaval of previous revolutions. It required no shift from one environment or one regime to another. It changed our very habits without our being entirely aware of the change. But change us it did, and the changes that this revolution has made – will make – to the way we live, are at least as important as its famous predecessor.

The question is, are we ready for those changes? Because they are already upon us, whether we realise it or not.

Boiling Frog Syndrome

How, you may ask, can a revolution take place around us without our being aware of it? The answer lies in the fact that the changes, though swift in historical terms, have been decades in the making and, as humans, we adapt to change almost without thinking about it.

We are like the famous frog in the infamous pan of water.

Drop a frog into boiling water, and it will attempt to leap out – naturally. But place it in a pan of cool water, and bring it slowly to the boil, and the creature will adjust to the changing temperature – and sit there until it cooks[ix].

Since the mid-Seventies, the world has changed around us, and we have adapted to the change – some of us more effectively than others. This is often referred to as Boiling Frog Syndrome.

But adapting is not the same as surviving, long-term.

Ask the frog!

So, what are these two revolutions we refer to? Here is a quick thumb nail sketch...

Revolution #1: The Industrial Revolution

The Industrial Revolution took off in Britain towards the end of the 18th Century with the invention of industrial machines, better tool-making and, most importantly, the steam engine. These inventions led to the creation of factories and mass transportation and a shift from an agricultural economy to an industrial one.

Until the 18th Century, all the moments of great achievement mentioned earlier, from Socrates and Plato to Da Vinci and Newton, had their effect on the intellectual life of their societies, but for the average citizen (or slave), life went on pretty much as it had always done.

The rich enjoyed fine art and architecture and scientists argued about the nature of the Universe, but everyday existence remained virtually unchanged. The life of the average person was still subject to the seasons, the cycles of famine or feast, and what a man could produce with his hands.

What made the Industrial Revolution a *revolution*, was the fact that it affected everyone. Almost overnight, in historical terms, society, as we had known it for endless centuries, was permanently changed.

People moved from the country to the city, working in the factories and offices and adapting to a totally new environment.

The revolution itself was over by the end of the 19th Century, but it lived on through the changes it had set in motion. Steam became internal-combustion, gas became electricity, the car was born, and the aeroplane and the refrigerator and the washing machine, and...

Industrial society continued to evolve and spread across the planet.

The Birth of the Consumer

It was not always a smooth transition – all revolutions involve social upheaval. Over time, however, the old ways were replaced with the new.

Mass production and mass marketing became the new universal model. The lights came on, what were once luxuries became, first affordable, then essential, and the consumer was born.

Life was comfortable – for those who were employed and/or lived in the right countries.

And universal mass education was introduced.

As a 19th Century innovation, tailored to the specific needs of industrial society, it served moderately well.

But then the second Revolution came along.....

Revolution #2: The Information Revolution

What are the origins of the Information Revolution?

As industrial society developed and trade expanded rapidly, a new class of citizen emerged: the office worker. Their job was to do paperwork and help businesses (and governments) keep track of their activities.

But success creates its own challenges. The paper-storm became an avalanche, and then a tsunami. A new way of storing and organising information was needed.

Around the same time, scientists were coming to terms with the shape of the cosmos, post-Einstein. They, too, needed a more efficient way of storing the data so that they could do the calculations, which explained an ever-expanding quantum universe.

Based on the work of brilliant pioneers like Britain's tragic genius Alan Turing, the answer to both problems arrived in the 1940s and 50s in the form of the computer.

Initially, it didn't seem like an answer at all. Computers could store masses of data and do calculations at lightning speed, but they were ridiculously expensive. And a single machine could take up the whole floor of an office-building.

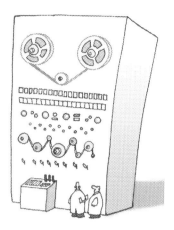

Still, the breakthrough had been made. Time and human ingenuity saw the replacement of these behemoths with smaller, faster, and vastly cheaper, machines.

And computers became easier to use.

Suddenly, a degree in computing or higher mathematics was no longer required to operate them – any child could do it.

The Birth of the Internet and the Global Village

Computers became indispensible in offices and research laboratories – and in many homes.

Then came the worldwide web and the search engine. Data could now be created, stored and (most critically, in terms of creating a universal revolution) **shared with others**. At the click of a button, people could communicate with each other – instantly and effortlessly.

Every computer which connected to the web was a two-way source of information, and as processing speeds and storage capacity (both on-site and on a remote server) increased, so did the volume of information available, expanding exponentially, until almost any information known to humans could be found – somewhere – almost as fast as you could type the request.

The internet was a reality and the 'global village'[x] predicted by futurists as early as the 1940's had sprung into existence. A world without borders was no longer an idealistic notion. At a cyber level, it was a *fait accompli*.

Today, your slim, palm-sized, data-enabled, blue-toothed and wi-fied, touch-screen smart-phone packs into its miniaturised circuits and its cloud-linked memory far more raw computing power than a 50s main-frame weighing tons – or the 'state-of-the-art'1960s computers that sent astronauts to the Moon.

Almost seamlessly, we have moved from the Machine Age to the Information Age.

The Information Revolution has arrived in all its kaleidoscopic glory, and its arrival has huge implications for our notions of education – for both the young and the not-so-young...

Chapter 2

Education in the Pre-Pentium Environment

Filling the Mind

Respected American educator Roland Barth wrote that 50 years ago, at their high-school graduation, students knew *'perhaps 75%'* of what they would need to know for the rest of their lives. Today, he suggests, they leave knowing perhaps 2%. *'The other 98% is yet to come.'*[xi]

It has been estimated that the sum of human knowledge is doubling every 2 to 2.5 years, and the pace is accelerating dramatically.

As far as education is concerned, the Information Revolution has shifted the goal-posts forever. While human beings are adaptable, however, their institutions are less so.

Around the world, education is struggling to prepare young people for life in the new century.

Monolithic national and state education systems tend to mirror the society they serve, but with societal change as rapid and wide-ranging as we have seen in recent years, it has become virtually impossible for them to keep pace.

Education systems across the planet are, effectively, one revolution behind; teaching for a world which has already passed into history.

Earlier, we said that universal mass education was a 19th Century innovation. It did not, however, come about through some altruistic belief that it should be the right of every child to have an education – though forward-thinking reformers, like England's William Wilberforce, did believe that way.

Universal education grew out of the need to have workers with at least enough education to function – in the factories and the offices.

A more educated workforce was regarded in much the same way as any other more refined raw material. Whatever improved the product or the efficiency of the production process was seen as a sound investment.

This was why 19th and early 20th Century mass education concentrated on the '3 Rs' – Reading, 'Riting and 'Rithmetic. A broader education was still the domain of the privileged classes.

Curriculum content was limited to what it was deemed necessary to know. This content was set, and delivered, by authority figures. Learning consisted of passively memorising given information with the aim of regurgitating it at a later date, and a minimum of critical analysis of what was being taught.

It consisted of all the information that a worker should ever need during the course of a lifetime.

Anything extra was up to the individual. It was, by definition, extra-curricular.

Although the scope of school curricula gradually broadened, the essential approach remained the same. It was an approach suited to a society where authority, both within the home and beyond, was there to be obeyed.

And it worked, for a period of time...

Chapter 3

Coping with the Evolution of Information Technologies in a Post-Pentium World

The Problem of Passive Learning

Today, we are in the midst of a significant global transition. New technologies have opened up a universe of information with infinite possibilities, but, sadly, we are still approaching this amazing resource with the old school mindset of passive learning.

In order to understand the limitations of traditional passive learning strategies, it is important to understand both the incredible strengths and the very real limitations of our remarkable human brain.

Many of our insights into the nature of the learning brain are recent – the result of breakthroughs during the last 20 or 30 years in the fields of neuroscience; cognitive psychology; information technology and even paleophysiology.

In the first of his celebrated Reith lectures[xii] in 2003, neuroscientist V.S. Ramachandran pointed out that with its 100 billion neurons, each capable of making up to ten thousand connections with other neurons, the human brain is arguably the universe's 'most complexly organised structure'[xiii].

The upshot of this incredible neural complexity is that the number of possible connections in an individual human brain – the number of different potential 'brain-states' – is, quite literally, astronomical: **100 billion to the power of ten thousand.**

This is a number so indescribably huge that it has been estimated to exceed 'the number of elementary particles in the known universe'[xiv].

Why is this number so important? Because it is through its ability to make these innumerable neural connections that the human brain is able to handle and store information, processes, habits, personality traits and all the other things which combine to make us thinking, functioning – and creative – human beings.

In computing terms, this ability to make connections and store information and 'programming' means that we possess, inside our skulls, an immense and powerful organic hard-drive. It is practically impossible to 'fill up' a human brain. Its plasticity (its ability to alter its own physical structure with the assimilation of each new learning) means that from before birth and throughout life it is constantly preparing itself for the next learning – which makes it the ideal tool for interpreting and coping with life in a rapidly-changing and sometimes dangerous environment.

It is what enabled a weak, slow and relatively defenceless creature to rise in the evolutionary hierarchy to rule a planet filled with creatures which, one-on-one, are faster, more aggressive, more ruthless and more physically dominant.

Human beings can learn; adapt quickly to new situations; use previous learning to facilitate new insights and create innovative solutions, and we owe it all to the unique ability of the human brain to physically remake itself – consistently and efficiently.

No computer yet invented has this unique ability to incrementally upgrade its own hardware.

Of course, like any tool, we must learn to use our brain effectively, if we are to make the most of its vast potential – but rarely, if ever, are our children trained in the best use of their incredible aptitudes.

Inside the learning brain, knowledge is scaffolded, then constructed, through a process which we will call 'narrative accumulation'[xv]. In formal terms, we define this as:

the integration of novel sensory input with existing narrative strings, through the association and sequential ordering of elements, into ever-more-complex narrative sequences, that reinforce understanding and facilitate recall, cross-association and creative innovation.[xvi]

Put simply, we learn by making connections and we can only effectively connect things which, at some level, we understand – that is, things which connect in a meaningful way with what we already know. Random facts and fragments simply don't stick, because it is harder to link them to our 'story' of the world. This is because, for all its vast computing power, the human brain also suffers from a major 'design flaw'.

To extend the computer analogy, while we possess a truly impressive hard-drive, the RAM of our on-board computer is, sadly, far less impressive.

From the 1950s to the 1990s, the seminal work of G.A. Miller, John Sweller and many others in the field of working memory and cognitive load limitation opened a window onto this inherent weakness, and the mechanisms that we, as a species, have evolved to overcome it. Today, neuroscience is beginning to look more closely at the neural mechanisms which explain the process.

The exact amount of information which we can hold in our working memory is subject to some heated debate, but scientists agree that, in comparison to the processing power and storage capacity of our cerebral cortex, it is tiny.

Since 1956[xvii], the 'magic number seven' (originally described as [7 +/- 2]) has been popularly accepted as the average number of elements that we can hold in our short-term memory and work with. Later work[xviii] looked at how we 'chunk' or structure information to better control it, and the debate over what constitutes a 'chunk' and how many of them we can handle at one time is on-going – but the essential fact remains.

Our ability to hold things in our conscious awareness and work with them is extremely limited.

We overcome our limitations by rapidly comparing, contrasting and linking new information with existing patterns commonly known as **schema**, (what we, in our new work, refer to as '***narrative constructs***'[xix]). These constructs are stored in the cerebral cortex – popularly referred to as the 'long-term' memory.

This process is non-conscious and highly efficient. It transforms unprocessed information into understanding, and enables us to use what we already know to help assimilate and manipulate the new information effectively.

The more we know, the more constructs we have to draw upon – and the more we can therefore learn.

But how do these 'narrative constructs' – these concepts – help us to overcome the cognitive load limitations we are born with? For the answer to this question, it is helpful to look at the work of the *Centre for the Mind* at the University of Sydney.

The *Centre for the Mind* was the brainchild of Emeritus Professor Allan Snyder – a ground-breaking, Marconi-Award-winning researcher, acknowledged as one of the most innovative scientific thinkers of the past 50 years. A Fellow of the Royal Society, he is a man who has made breakthroughs in four different fields and we are proud to have collaborated with him for more than 15 years, to give his pioneering research practical application in the world of education.

One of Allan Snyder's key areas of research is 'concept formation' – specifically, what happens in the brain, when we form a concept. He began by working with autistic savants, and what he discovered was that while savants could process masses of detail extremely quickly, they were generally unable to conceptualise – to generalise an understanding from the mass of detail; to find the 'narrative' that linked the elements together into a coherent understanding. This meant that though they had a privileged access to 'information that resides equally in everyone, but cannot normally be accessed'[xx], they could make no use of it.

In a series of elegant experiments[xxi], using trans-cranial magnetic stimulation (TMS) to part of a subject's left fronto-temporal lobe, Snyder was able to dampen, temporarily, activity in the part of the brain responsible for forming and utilising concepts. Within minutes, subjects (including one of the authors) were able to demonstrate an increased awareness of detail in tasks such as drawing and proof-reading.

The results showed that, though we do not normally have the savant's privileged access to the details, those details are still there, stored in our long-term memory. As one of the papers states:

> *We see the whole, not the parts. The details are inhibited when the concept network is activated, ie. the inhibition is dynamic and can be switched on and off. Autism is suggested to be the state of retarded concept formation.*[xxii]

This research is of vital importance to our understanding of cognitive load limitation and the brain's inherent ability to overcome it. We control the mass of detail, and stop it overwhelming our limited working memory, by instinctively forming concepts, then automatically inhibiting conscious access to the details, thus freeing up invaluable space on the 'desktop' of our on-board computer.

Later experiments using transcranial direct current stimulation (tDCS)[xxiii] had an even more spectacular effect on the subjects' responses – notably, their ability to solve a previously 'unsolvable' problem, known as the 'nine dot' problem. In the experiment none of the subjects could solve the problem prior to the stimulation, but after 10 minutes of stimulation designed to dampen activity in the part of the brain involved in the creation and use of concepts, 40% of subjects were able to access a novel and creative solution – to quite literally 'think outside the box'.

Understanding this process – and particularly the 'narrative' nature of concepts – has huge implications for the structuring of school curricula and the development of 'brain-friendly' learning and creativity strategies, and this has been the focus of much of our work with Professor Snyder for over a decade and a half.

Here is a simple example of cognitive load limitation in action, taken from our school days. We used to call it 'mental arithmetic'.

Look at the following addition sum for five seconds, then look away and calculate the answer in your head:

$$23$$
$$+\underline{35}$$

The answer, of course, is **58**. And you probably didn't need the full five seconds.

We can do this calculation in our heads, because the number of elements involved is only 5 (4 integers and a '+' sign). Let's call this a cognitive load of 5. (Measurement of cognitive load is a little more complex than this, but for our current purposes, this will suffice.)

We can hold all 5 elements in our working memory and do the calculation simultaneously – but here is the interesting thing. Even in an example as simple as this, we can already see the complex mechanisms of cognition at work.

In our pre-learned, pre-stored 'narrative' of numbers, the position of the numbers and the '+' sign have an intrinsic meaning. We don't have to think about it consciously, because they are subconsciously linked to a process (called 'addition') which we stored in the procedural memory around the age of 5 or 6 – a process which kicks in automatically and efficiently in response to the specific pattern presented.

Would the solution have come as easily, if the elements had been presented without the familiar structure?

Almost certainly not. No pattern, no process.

Now, let's try overloading the working memory and see what happens. Take five seconds to look at the next sum, then look away and try to calculate the answer in your head.

13,542,874
29,810,982
+11,322,456

The answer is **54,676,312**, and, if it were written down in front of us, we could all work it out quite easily using a pencil, but very few individuals in the world could do that simple calculation in their heads.

Why? Because, with 8 integers in each row, as well as the '+' sign, we have 25 elements (or a cognitive load more than 3 times the capacity of the working memory). It's like trying to load too much into your computer's RAM. The system simply freezes.

We can't hold all the elements in conscious awareness and manipulate them – even using familiar and automated processes. The cognitive load is simply too large.

Really?

Well, what about this challenge? On the next line is a task containing 26 elements – one more than the previous 'impossible' sum. Your job is to look at it for just 3 seconds, then close the book and write down, or type, as many of the elements – in order – as you can.

A B C D E F G H I J K L M N O P Q R S T U V W X Y Z

Could you do it? Of course you could. It was so elementary that you probably didn't even bother to. And yet, the raw cognitive load, in terms of the number of individual elements, was even higher than the previous example.

Of course, the reason you could do it is that you recognised the pattern. 'The Alphabet.'

A cursory glance, and the 26 elements became 1. The letters were still there, but somewhere in your preschool years, you internalised the sequence which we use to tame them.

And how did you learn that pattern? Probably with a song.

For your developing brain, the song, with its engaging tune, its rhymes and rhythms, engaged you and reduced a load of 26 elements to just 4 memorable patterns:

A B C D E F G
H I J K L M N O P
Q R S T U V
W X Y and Z

and, once learned, the patterns gradually became a single concept: the alphabet.

Armed with that concept, we can use a dictionary to find a word; we can arrange random elements into alphabetical order and a thousand other tasks – but take away the pattern, and the complexity returns.

Let's prove it.

After looking at the following line for just 3 seconds, could you write or type it out accurately?

M N B V C X Z A S D F G H J K L P O I U Y T R E W Q

Not quite so easy, is it? Removing the familiar pattern means that we are again faced with 26 random elements, and the task becomes virtually impossible – except for a certain kind of savant.

Unless, of course, we provide a clue that gives the elements a conceptual structure – a narrative. The letters are **the QWERTY keyboard typed backwards**, beginning at the bottom right and travelling right to left, left to right, then right to left again along the 3 lines of letters.

Now, armed with that narrative – the concept of the keyboard backwards – could you type out the 26 letters in the correct order? Of course. It is the pattern – the concept – and our ability to internalise it that gives it meaning and overcomes the flaws in our design.

Active learning, especially in young, inexperienced brains, uses context and experiential interaction with environmental information sources (known as play) to help the brain make the necessary connections – to create the narratives – that tie new learnings to existing ones.

Traditional passive learning, on the other hand, focusses on the gaining and storage of discreet information – either through drill and rote-learning, or through other approaches designed to capture that information for later retrieval.

The incremental construction of an internal body of 'knowledge' has been the main thrust of educational programs and strategies for centuries, but the 21st Century demands a new model – one more in tune with how the brain operates most effectively.

Leading the Mind

The human mind is driven to learn and, as we have seen, it does this by making its own connections. This is a genetic imperative.

The brain detects a pattern or a narrative sequence in the flood of sensory inputs surrounding it, and compares it, at lightning speed, with the millions of patterns and sequences already stored in memory. If it perceives a match, it interprets the new information through the existing filter and creates, through association, a new understanding or idea. We call this process imagination.

And our imagination loves to be led. This is why you can sit in a dark room with 300 strangers and be moved to laughter or tears by images on a screen. When the lights go out, they can project a cartoon picture of a fish, give it a name – like Nemo or Dory – and millions of families around the world will buy popcorn and flock to see it.

While our logical brain knows that the cartoon fish is not real, our imagination is led to connect with the deeper values which the film expresses. The same principle holds for all great forms of Art – including teaching.

The media and the game manufacturers understand the power of leading the imagination. For their own purposes, they lure children into a stimulating visual, auditory and interactive environment, which is, for most young people, infinitely more enticing than a traditional teacher-centred classroom.

This has been the case since the invention of the radio and the television, of course, but it is becoming far more prevalent, invasive and pernicious since the emergence of the internet, electronic gaming and the social media.

Never before has a generation grown up with such intense sensory stimulation at such an early age, focussing for hours at a time on a small square of colourful moving images, with sound wired directly into their ears and haptic feedback vibrating against sensitive nerve-endings. Is it any wonder that they find it hard to sit still and stare at Chapter 14? Nothing on the page is moving. Where is the stimulation?

The imagination craves stimulation, and we can use that fundamental human drive to lead children into a new world of discovery and wonder – but only if we understand it.

Only if we are willing to change, along with the new world we have set in motion.

The information game has changed radically but, most of the time, we still expect our children to play by the old rules.

And at what cost?

As parents and educators, it is our duty to understand the mindset demanded by the world of the Information Revolution. We need to create a whole new generation of active learners. People who, armed with a positive attitude, are confident enough to engage with what they are learning.

And why do we need this change of approach so urgently?

Because our relationship with information has changed irrevocably and our systems have no choice but to change along with it.

Either we learn to ride the wave of change, or we risk being swamped by it.

Diamond Rain Revisited

Albert Einstein hit upon his most creative theories through the use of elaborate thought experiments. His Theory of Relativity came about when he imagined himself riding on the end of a beam of light.

We began our discussion of the 3-Mind Revolution with our own thought experiment. By imagining diamond rain, we can examine the effect of over-supply on the value of diamonds.

A diamond is a universal symbol of value. Just ask anyone about to get engaged! But what, exactly, makes it valuable?

Is it its hardness? Perhaps, but industrial diamonds are the only ones actually used for their hardness, and they aren't considered particularly valuable.

Perhaps it is its clarity, colour and cut – isn't that the line that the jeweller feeds you, when he explains why the diamond you 'just have to have' is worth over three and a half months' salary?

Actually, the value of a diamond has little to do with its clarity or its beauty. If aesthetics were the deciding factor, wouldn't a cubic zirconia be worth just as much? Few people can really tell the difference.

The true source of a diamond's value is much more basic – and unromantic.

Diamonds are valuable simply because they are perceived to be rare. A point not lost on diamond traders.

Regardless of how many diamonds are mined in a given year, the actual supply is strictly controlled. This ensures scarcity so that demand remains high.

The value of any commodity – whether it be diamonds, or cow manure – is dependent upon a symbiotic relationship between its availability and how desperately, or otherwise, people want or need it. This fundamental principle of economics is known as 'supply and demand'.

In a world of diamond rain, diamonds are universally available and are, therefore, universally worthless.

They could still be used for jewellery, of course, because their aesthetic value would remain undiminished. Their commercial value however would be wiped out.

The rules governing the value of information are no different.

Before the Information Revolution, accessible information was relatively scarce. Books were expensive, libraries were often under-funded, a mouse was a small rodent and a button was something you used to fasten your coat – not something you 'clicked'.

Back then, what I could memorise and store in my brain was of real worth. It was how I added value to my brain – and, therefore, to myself as a potential employee.

Fifty years ago, if my father travelled overseas and brought back the latest reference books, I would be considered lucky. Twenty years ago, if a country had well-stocked public libraries, its citizens had the right to feel privileged.

Today, a child is considered egregiously *under*privileged if he doesn't have access to the sum total of the world's knowledge via the internet. We've come a long way in one lifetime!

Previously, when applying for a job, I could press my case by proving **what I knew** – the facts and the figures – in the form of my graduation certificate.

If what I knew met the employer's needs, I had the job. Often, for life.

But no longer…

The Law of Supply and Demand

Information, like any other commodity, is subject to the laws of supply and demand. Look at this graph.

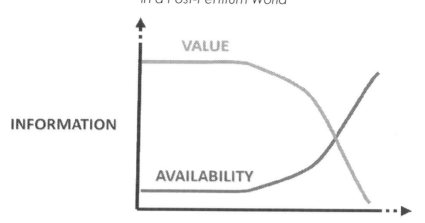

Just like diamonds, the more available information becomes, the less it is worth.

And with everything we need to know (and a lot that we don't!) available at the click of a button, raw information is now of little commercial value – no matter how much time and effort (and money) it cost me to lodge it in my brain!

Today, a young woman, playing by the old rules, enters a job interview armed with a certificate and a headful of facts that she has spent the past few years assiduously learning.

"This is what I know," she says – as her father and mother did before her. But, sadly for her, things have changed. The employer asks her a question – which she answers quickly and accurately. He then leans across the desk, clicks on a search engine and comes up with a more detailed and up-to-date version of exactly the same answer.

"Hmmm," he says. "I know that too. Why should I pay **you** for information that I, or any of my staff, can easily access for nothing?"

This is not to say that there is suddenly no value in learning as much as we possibly can. As we will soon see, there is always value in internalising knowledge. The question is not **whether** we should learn as much as possible, but rather, *'How efficient are our methods of actively comprehending and storing that knowledge?'* because this has a crucial bearing on how we can use it effectively later on.

In a rapidly-changing environment, our capacity for innovative thinking and the quality of our creative problem-solving are being constantly tested.

Professor Snyder's original studies into creativity focussed, in the most part, on the development of a Creativity Quotient (CQ) – a measure of an individual's potential for creativity. Our work, in collaboration with him, focussed on the development of CQ measurements for young people. This research suggested numerous strategies for enhancing and developing the creative potential in all our students. It is an example of what can be achieved, when research and practical, real-world application go hand-in-hand.

In a 2004 paper[xxiv], Snyder proposed a more accurate way of measuring creative potential by plotting a person's creative responses using an algorithm based on two distinct criteria – known as 'ideational fluency' and 'ideational flexibility'.

In simple terms, it showed that we can measure a person's CQ far more effectively if we look at two things:

i) How many solutions they can think of to a given problem – say, 'List all the possible uses for a piece of paper.' This measure is known as 'ideational fluency', and

ii) How many distinct semantic categories those solutions are drawn from – which is known as 'ideational flexibility'.

In terms of solutions, writing a letter, drawing a diagram and writing a poem/essay/shopping-list etc. would all be considered examples of the same semantic category – 'marking the paper' – but creating an origami swan; lighting a fire; using paper as insulation or as a torture instrument, or crushing it into a ball and playing soccer with it would be seen as examples of different categories, and ranked higher.

If creativity is a combination of fluency and flexibility, then the more concepts and categories I hold in my head already, the more disparate associative connections I can make and the more potential I have for truly creative thought.

Even a cursory study of creativity reveals that the more knowledge domains we have experience in, the more fluent and flexible our creativity becomes. A solid knowledge base is essential in order to innovate and solve problems, and our ability to comprehend new concepts is extremely limited, unless we can make meaningful connections between the different types of knowledge within this base.

So, the Information Revolution has not negated the need to learn 'facts'. To the contrary, it has intensified the need to learn – **but at a higher level**. What the internet has done, is to completely rewrite the rules regarding **how** and **why** we learn.

Learning today requires the active understanding of concepts, not the passive absorption of facts, because understanding facilitates connection and connection facilitates both imagination and creativity – which, as we will see later, are not the same thing.

We are no longer paid for our knowledge. We are paid for what we can **do** with that knowledge at a moment's notice. We are required to apply knowledge to solve problems and innovate.

Today our importance to an employer is dependent upon:

    i)   our interpersonal skills, our communication abilities and our mindset.

ii)   our ability to control the endless information-flow and isolate the relevant factors, and

iii)   our creativity

Chapter 4

Preparing for the World of Tomorrow

Understanding the Game

Whether we are educating infants, children and young people, or re-educating ourselves, preparation for the 21st Century needs to be effective in these three key areas:

i) **Social**

The 21st Century work-place has moved from a competitive, hierarchy-based model, to a more collaborative, team-based one.

To function effectively in cooperation with others and with a healthy personal ecology, we must each develop:

- communication skills,
- emotional intelligence,
- self-awareness,
- confidence,

  and

- a Champion Mindset (the ability to embrace our own unique talents, differentiate ourselves, and learn from adversity)

These are all skills that can be taught and learned. Until now, however, they have generally not been adequately addressed by education systems worldwide.

Teaching children to debate is not the same as teaching them to communicate, any more than drilling for a spelling bee guarantees improvement in their love for the language. It can occur, of course – and has throughout the centuries – but it often occurs in spite of, not because of, the training.

ii) Educational

We began this book by quoting Marshall McLuhan's famous maxim, *'the medium is the message'*, and half a century on, his words still ring true. Our children are immersed in the media that surround them, and any educational strategies we devise must be based on the realisation that today **how** we learn is at least as important as **what** we learn.

From this perspective, the Information Revolution has changed the rules of education forever.

The old world emphasised the drill and rote-learning of masses of given information, and testing procedures which focussed on the correct answers to specific questions.

The 19th/20st Century Model of Learning

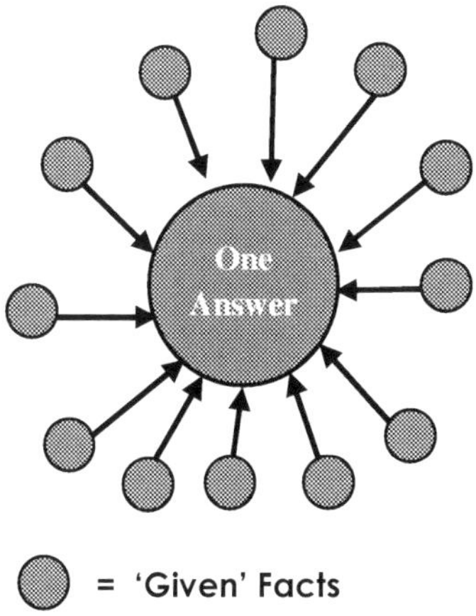

One
Answer

⬤ = 'Given' Facts

The new world requires an emphasis on learning processes and information control strategies.

Education that is more suited to this world instils skills and strategies rather than drilling facts. Students are asked for solutions to a given problem or the consequences of a specific course of action, rather than mere recall.

21st Century Model of Learning

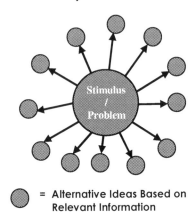

= Alternative Ideas Based on Relevant Information

iii) **Creative**

These days we have to constantly develop innovative solutions and this means that we have to be creative.

In most developed countries, with the advent of globalisation, automation and computerisation, the process-worker model is rapidly becoming a relic of the industrial past. Sometimes we will be asked to work creatively as individuals, but more commonly we will have to be creative as part of a team.

The 'Process-Worker' Model	The 'Collaborative Creativity' Model

Creativity has rules and strategies – a 'craft' that can be taught.

Creativity Education should be a vital part of building every 21st Century citizen.

Social, Educational, Creative...

The **3-Mind Revolution** grew from this basic understanding of 21st Century needs...

*

A Trinity of Minds: Learning Into the Future

In 1624 poet and philosopher John Donne wrote:

'*No man is an island, entire of itself...*'[xxv]

What was true in the 17th Century is even more relevant today. Our digital technologies currently link us to billions of other human beings across the entire globe – even if we are not consciously aware of their individual existence. This web of social, intellectual, cultural and commercial commonality rapidly dismantles the popular notion that six degrees of separation distance us from any other person on the planet.

'Six degrees of separation' means that, on average, an acquaintance or friendship chain of no more than six steps, is all that is needed to connect any individual in the world to any other person in the world.

By way of example, if Hector met Brianna, who had once done the make-up for Sir Elton John, who met the Queen of England when he received his knighthood, then Hector would be separated from the Queen by only three degrees of separation, but if Clarissa knew Lucy, whose brother, Fred once went to school with Hector, then the distance for Clarissa would be six degrees.

Without considering YouTube, Twitter, Linkedin, instagram and every commercial marketing organisation which has, legitimately or otherwise, come into possession of our myriad contact details, if we just focus on the social network colossus, Facebook, the organisation's own internal research project reveals an interesting snapshot of the world-shrinking effect of social networking.

In 2011, when the site had 721 million users, the average 'distance' between users was just 4.74 degrees of separation, down from a reported 5.28 degrees in 2008[xxvi]. In February 2016, when the number of users had reached 1.6 billion (about 22% of the world's population) the average distance had further decreased to a remarkable 3.57 degrees[xxvii].

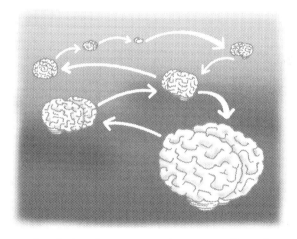

The concept of six degrees of separation has been in existence since 1929, when there were only about two billion people in the entire world. It was the brainchild of Hungarian Frigyes Karinthy, but was subsequently studied by numerous researchers, who generally found the average to be in the 'six degrees' vicinity.

Now, the world population exceeds seven billion (reaching that milestone somewhere between October 2011 and March 2012 – depending on your information source), yet the average distance between us and any of the 7+ billion inhabitants of this vast planet – through Facebook alone – is now just 3.57 acquaintances. Add the other on-line networks into the mix, and the number is likely to be significantly lower still.

In terms of connection, if the 'distance' between people is diminishing, then the distance separating the knowledge we control and share has all but evaporated. Between the social networks; Wikipedia; YouTube; business networking sites like Linkedin; the ubiquitous commercial websites; professional networks; Amazon and Kindle and a million other, readily available sites, our level of separation, in terms of information, is probably less than three degrees – one or two clicks of a mouse button, and the world lies open before us.

And students are far more comfortable with this concept than are most of their teachers.

The problem comes, when we need to sift through the morass of information to find the nuggets of truth, or more importantly, the relevant knowledge for the task at hand – whatever that may be.

In the Introduction, we quoted the wisdom of futurist Alvin Toffler:

> *The illiterate of the 21st Century will not be those who cannot read and write, but those who cannot learn, unlearn and relearn.*

Today, we live in Toffler's prophetically conceived future: a constantly evolving and terminally confusing world.

In this brave, new world, the ability to cope with change will mark the difference between success and failure.

This means developing three distinct minds:

    i)   **The Champion Mind,**

    ii)   **The Learning Mind**

             and

    iii)   **The Creative Mind**

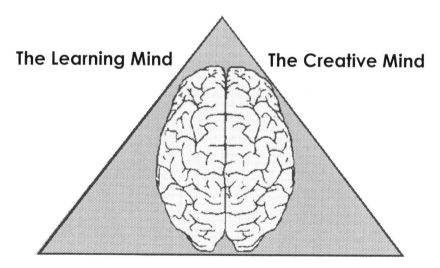

The Learning Mind   **The Creative Mind**

The Champion Mind

This trinity of minds is the foundation of the **3-Mind Revolution.**

If we are to negotiate our way successfully through our exciting new world, all the three minds need to develop in unison.

So, let's look at each one in turn...

Chapter 5

Mind #1: The Champion Mind

Charlie Brown vs Linus

Charles M. Schultz, the creator of the *Peanuts* comic strip was famous for his insight into what it means to be human and fallible. That was what made his creations so popular and endearing.

In the first of the animated *Peanuts* feature cartoons[xxviii], Charlie Brown, Lucy and Linus are lying on a hilltop watching the sky.

"Aren't the clouds beautiful?" says Lucy. "They look like big balls of cotton. I can just lie here all day and watch them drift by. If you use your imagination, you can see lots of things in the cloud formations. What do you think you see, Linus?"

Linus, being Linus, replies, "Well, those clouds up there look to me like the map of the British Honduras, on the Caribbean... That cloud up there, looks a little like the profile of Thomas Eakins, the famous painter and sculptor... And that group of clouds over there reminds me of the Stoning of Stephen. I can see the apostle Paul standing there to one side."

Then it is Charlie Brown's turn, but when Lucy asks him, "What do you see in the clouds, Charlie Brown?" he hesitates.

"Well..." he says, finally, "I was going to say I saw a duck and a horsey, but I changed my mind."

Linus clearly has an active imagination – which we will return to later – but let's look at Charlie Brown's reaction. Is it the reaction of a champion?

Perhaps not.

Research from the Centre for the Mind demonstrates that champions are people who don't hesitate to express their individuality. These individuals find unique strengths within themselves and use them to advantage, even if this means going against accepted wisdom.

Even if doing so makes them stand out and exposes them to criticism or ridicule.

Linus has the confidence to express his vision, regardless of what others may see. In this, he displays a key characteristic of the Champion Mind.

Charlie Brown, however...

Perhaps a duck and a horsey are not as 'impressive' as Linus' diverse imaginings, but they are no less valid. There are no right and wrong answers to Lucy's question – only clouds, passing overhead like a cotton wool Rorschach test.

Charlie Brown's lack of championship lies, not in the simplicity of his response, but in the fact that he refuses to embrace and broadcast it confidently.

He lacks one key ingredient of the Champion Mind – the confidence to trust in his own unique vision.

Out of the Box: The Anatomy of the Champion Mind

The Champion Mind is a way of thinking which prepares the individual, mentally, for success.

It is built from equal parts of:

i) emotional intelligence,

ii) communication skills,

iii) self-awareness

and

iv) self-confidence

Champion Mindset is another area of ground-breaking research undertaken, over the last 20 years, by Professor Snyder. Its basic elements were outlined in his seminal book, *What Makes a Champion!* in 2002.

Championship, in the broadest sense of the word – being the best that you can be in all aspects of your life – is a quality of mind that we too have been intensely interested in since the late nineties, and our close collaboration with Professor Snyder has enabled us to develop strategies for inculcating the Champion Mindset in young people.

Snyder is indelibly linked with the 'Champion Mindset' – in fact it was he who coined the term. He also made the telling observation that:

> *In the best of times the Champion Mindset is a valuable commodity; in the worst of times it is an absolute necessity.*[xxix]

His breakthrough discovery is that the Champion Mindset is not some mysterious quality only present in a few lucky individuals. His research clearly demonstrates that the key elements of a Champion Mindset can actually be *learned*.

Snyder studied champions worldwide through events such as his spectacularly successful 'What Makes a Champion?' forum in conjunction with the Sydney 2000 and the Beijing 2008 Olympic Games. Through this study, he demonstrated a truth that is both simple and profound.

If you want to understand championship, you must put aside the rhetoric of the motivational speakers: the drive to succeed; the power of positive thinking and visualisation; perseverance and the will to win. These attributes are all obvious and without them you will never succeed in achieving your goals in the modern world.

But drive and visualisation will take you only so far. Without the mindset of a champion, you will always remain in the ranks of the 'also-rans', regardless of how many motivational courses you've attended.

Because championship is not limited to the sporting arena, Professor Snyder studied international champions from many diverse fields. These included scientists, business leaders and entrepreneurs, Olympic gold-medallists, spiritual leaders, artists, diplomats, writers, philanthropists, politicians, Oscar-winners, and Nobel Laureates.

Subjects included renowned individuals such as Nelson Mandela, Sir Edmund Hillary, Sir Richard Branson, Oliver Sacks, and the Dalai Lama.

The result of all this research is a simple list of three intrinsic qualities that set champions apart from the rest.

1. **Champions abhor being ordinary.** They make a conscious decision to identify what is unique about themselves and broadcast it. In this way, they leave their individual mark on everything that they do.

2. **Champions are willing to transcend conventional wisdom.** If the old way doesn't work they quickly find a new way.

3. **Champions also develop the ability to accept and learn from adversity.** This is referred to as 'converting upsets into set-ups'[xxx].

Championship means deciding to climb out of the box that society has placed us in.

Our school systems, with their top-down approach, discipline strategies and uniforms, strongly encourage group identity.

Then, when children step outside the school gates and into the real world, we expect them to suddenly become original and creative.

How can we expect this of children if they haven't been adequately prepared – if, neurologically, they have been pre-programmed for a very different response?

Many schools stress conformity both in terms of behaviour and in their approach to learning.

Strategically, in such schools, it is often better to remain safe and obtain a good pass mark than to take the risk of trying something different – and failing.

Learning from Adversity

Citizens of the 21st Century need a completely new attitude to failure and adversity. We should be helping our children (and retraining ourselves) to develop the mindset, and the ability, to treat a mistake – or even a catastrophe – as a valuable learning experience.

If we do this for our children, they will learn – without our help – to grow from it. If we do it for ourselves, we too will grow. It is never too late to learn this fundamental lesson.

As Professor Snyder points out, it is only through confronting adversity – and failure – that the Champion Mindset is forged.

Playing it safe and regurgitating information may result in high academic marks, but it is poor preparation for life in a rapidly-evolving world. After all, what is perceived as correct changes daily and the ability to respond positively to setbacks has become crucial.

Professor Snyder writes:

> *"Many of the world's greatest scientists were, at best, average students... Those who learn effortlessly in youth may well be at a disadvantage [later in life] in tackling seemingly insurmountable problems."*[xxxi]

Too many schools, acting in the role of tacit enforcers of conformity, neither adequately encourage, nor reward, such resilience – nor a child's willingness to think outside the box.

Here is a quote from the teacher of someone you may have heard of, informing that student's parents of his potential. Can you guess who this 'hopeless' child was? *(Answer at the end of the chapter.)*

'It doesn't matter what he does, he'll never amount to anything.'

Here is some food for thought...

Question: Apart from being male and being household names, what do Albert Einstein, Steven Spielberg, Sir Richard Branson and Apple co-founder Steve Jobs have in common?

Answer: Each was considered less than outstanding at school, in spite of his later achievements.

No one would deny that each of these phenomenally successful men has contributed to his society in a significant way, so why were they not outstanding in school?

Looking at their later lives:

- Did each man have a Champion Mind? – Most certainly.

- Did each man have a Learning Mind? – Clearly they did.

- Did each man have a Creative Mind? – Absolutely.

- Did the system recognise and support their championship, intelligence and creativity? – Apparently not!

Answer to the Question on Page 84 :

The 'hopeless' student in question was Albert Einstein!

In what must go down as one of the least perceptive comments in the history of parent-teacher interviews, the teacher in question offered this assessment of the potential of one of the world's most famous scientific and mathematical geniuses to Einstein's father in 1895.

Chapter 6

Mind #2: The Learning Mind

Aristotle, one of the most famous teachers in the history of the world, is reported to have said:

> *If you study to remember, you will forget, but if you study to understand, you will remember – for all Men, by nature, desire to know.*

Over the past 30 years, science has learned much about how the brain lays down memory, and everything that we now know supports what Aristotle observed over 2,000 years ago – without the aid of an fMRI machine!

> *All Men [and Women, and Children – and even Babies], by nature, desire to know...*

...not to pass some meaningless exam, not because their neighbour's kid got 'A's, not even because it may get them a good job in the future – but because it is human nature to **want** to understand. It's a part of our neurological make-up. It's programmed into our DNA.

The reason why mammals survived the Chicxulub impact was because they were more adaptable to change, and at least part of the reason for that adaptability lies in the fact that a mammal's brain is fundamentally different from the brains of reptiles, amphibians, fish or even birds.

Insects are very adaptable too, of course, but it has nothing to do with their miniscule brains. Insects are adaptable because they have a short life-span and have numerous offspring, enabling naturally-occurring mutations to swiftly produce favourable adaptations, generation after rapid generation, in the face of changing environmental conditions.

Mammals, on the other hand, are capable of changing their behaviour **within** their own life-times and as a result of experience, rather than waiting for a genetic mutation to fortuitously kick-start the change in some future generation. This is something pretty unique in the animal kingdom, and it is a result of the fact that – unlike reptiles, fish, amphibians, insects, and (probably) dinosaurs – mammals have emotions.

In the evolutionary card-game, scoring emotions was the equivalent of receiving a royal flush on the first deal – when everyone else had nothing better than low pairs.

You see, emotions are, essentially, the key to all learning.

All incoming sensory data is processed by the limbic system – which is the seat of emotion, as well as acting as an information clearing house and the first stage in the process of creating memories. We share this in common with all mammals, though, of course, the human limbic system and its capacity for information processing is infinitely more advanced than, say, a mouse, or even a dog.

And what about a lizard? Well, a lizard is a reptile, and reptiles rarely learn anything. The reptilian brain is born with every reflex, every response, hard-wired in. Without the processing power of the limbic system and the cortex, all its tiny brain can do is run its pre-programmed responses, unable to alter behaviour to accommodate changing conditions.

If a lizard runs into your kitchen and touches the hot stove, it will feel pain and run away, but if it comes again, there will be no memory of the incident and it is just as likely to make the same mistake – again and again, until it dies.

A mouse, on the other hand, though its emotions are far less developed than ours, has a significantly different response. When it burns itself, it feels two things: the pain – and fear. It is the fear that is the source of learning – if learning is defined as changing behaviour in response to a remembered stimulus. The experience, along with the emotion is transferred to the mouse's tiny cortex and stored.

Mice are slow learners. It may take a number of painful experiences for the learning to cement itself, but eventually, as the mouse approaches the stove and feels the radiated heat, the fear stored with the primitive memory kicks in before the pain is experienced, and the mouse runs away unhurt.

This emotion-based learning does not replace hard-wired danger responses, but it does augment them, giving the mouse a survival advantage over its reptilian counterpart.

We are far smarter than a mouse, of course, and the processing power of our amazing brains allows us to learn quickly and effectively, but despite our evolutionary advantages, we still lay down memories in pretty much the same way as a little brown rodent.

Information enters the limbic system and is stored temporarily (largely in the hippocampus) until it is assimilated into existing neural constructs, whereupon it passes into long-term storage in the cortex. The upshot of this arrangement is that emotion and learning are inextricably intertwined.

Why is this important? Because how we feel when we learn something strongly influences our future experience of the learning. Things learned under a cloud of fear, anxiety, shame, anger or frustration will generate echoes of those emotions every time the learning is accessed, and as we are naturally repelled by such negative feelings, we become reluctant to revisit the learning.

Learnings that are associated with happiness, safety, love, acceptance and confidence link us to feelings we are happy to revisit, so our relationship to the learning is a positive one.

Mastery of anything creates a feeling of contentment, fuelled by endorphins – Mother Nature's natural high. It makes us happy, and all the psychological and educational research – from Abraham Maslow sixty years agoxxxii to Martin Seligman and the Positive Psychology movement of the present dayxxxiii – points to the intimate connection between our emotions and our ability to learn and remember.

Put simply, happy people learn better than unhappy people – which is hardly rocket-science. What is not so well-known, however, is that certain types of learning make us happier – and therefore help us to learn more effectively.

It should come as no surprise that traditional 'drill-and-kill' strategies are not what we are talking about here.

The crammed-curriculum learning model is **disconnected from the natural learning process**. And it dries up the endorphins, because it's simply no fun to go against nature.

As human beings, we developed our learning processes through evolution – it is a part of our DNA. Think right back to the earliest cavemen and how they learned...

They learned by interacting with their environment. They came upon problems and solved them – or they died. They noticed connections and created stories or cave-art about them, so that they could pass on what they had learned. They experimented to carve better tools or improve the hunt, and passed on the insights. They developed stories, play and religion. These and other activities constituted their education system.

Well, the human brain has not essentially changed in well over 100,000 years. It is still wired to learn in pretty much the same way.

And, perhaps surprisingly, a less-structured education based partly upon this more ancient way of learning is actually more suited to the demands of our rapidly-evolving modern world, than the limited and artificial, 19th Century industrial model.

Watch young children at play.

It is through play and engagement that they learn to make sense of their world. In children, play supplies two of the most basic human needs – the need for happiness and the need for understanding; for making sense of a complex world.

But as we grow, surely there is no time for play. The world is a serious place, and there is too much to be done to waste time enjoying ourselves.

Intuitively, this may sound logical, but don't be too quick to embrace the notion that seriousness and learning must inevitably go together – even for adults.

Industrial society encouraged a narrow, functional learning model. By mastering the necessary stuff, you were preparing for your future function. You memorised the facts by sheer hard work, and gained your reward sometime in the future, in the form of a good job [translation: an activity which you worked hard at to earn enough to feed, clothe and house your family].

Enjoyment had little or nothing to do with the model.

Unfortunately, what is functional in one environment can rapidly become dysfunctional in another. For an environment in flux, education and learning habits must equip the individual for change – with the ability to 'join the dots' in new and more effective ways.

As we said earlier, our role, as 21st Century parents and educators can be summed up as creating a positive relationship with learning. We want all learners – children and adults – to have both a love of discovery for its own sake, and the skills to discern which information is useful, and which is not.

Think back to *Peanuts*. In the extract we looked at earlier, both boys 'saw' elements of their familiar worlds in the clouds.

What was the difference?

Charlie Brown, with limited experience, and a less adventurous relationship with learning, was constrained in his responses.

As a result, his imagination supplied 'a duck and a horsey'.

Linus, on the other hand, was able to draw examples from the worlds of Geography, Fine Arts and Bible History – an impressive combination, grounded in an enthusiastic relationship with learning.

On Professor Snyder's CQ rating, both his fluency and his flexibility would rate very highly.

Is Linus showing off? Quite possibly.

Does it set him apart? Most certainly. But as we have already seen, champions are not afraid to stand out from the crowd. In fact they live for it!

It's a fair bet, however, that Linus didn't learn about British Honduras, Thomas Eakins or Saint Stephen and Saint Paul in his Elementary School curriculum.

More important, however, is the fact that the knowledge he draws upon is clearly **a part of him**. Rather than rote-learned facts, these were things Linus was drawn to through natural curiosity.

Even half a century ago, Schultz' Linus was a character with a Learning Mind well-equipped for life in the 21st Century.

*

The Hourglass Model: Training the Learning Mind

Having spent our formative years in Australia, we have both been influenced by that country's national obsession with sports.

During the 2004 Athens Olympics, we found ourselves sitting together, watching the exploits of some of Australia's sporting heroes.

For a country with a relatively small population, Australia's performance in international sporting competitions is impressive. Diving, however, is one sport in which there has been a conspicuous lack of success, historically. China and the US have dominated diving for decades.

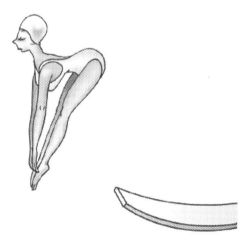

Imagine our surprise, then, to see two Australian girls taking on the world's best and winning. Australia did remarkably well in the 10-metre platform event winning both the gold and bronze medals.

After the gold-medallist Chantelle Newbery realized that she had won, she leapt in the air and ran over to hug her coaches.

And suddenly everything made sense.

Both her head coach, Hui Tong, and her senior coach, Wang Tong Xiang, were Chinese.

The Australian girls were both excellent divers. Natural talent and years of dedicated training had brought them to a world-class level. But this in itself was not enough. In order to win a gold medal, the Australian girls needed the extra edge that only the world's best technique can provide.

This was why the Australian diving team had gone to the country with the best technique to find its coaches.

The Australian diving success continued at the 2008 Beijing Olympics and the 2012 London Games. In Beijing, Matthew Mitcham won a gold in the men's 10-metre platform event, and the women's synchronised diving pair, Briony Cole and Melissa Wu, won silver, and in London, Brittany Broben won silver in the 10-metre platform, narrowly losing to the dominant Chinese diver, Chen Ruolin.

Clear evidence that better technique makes a huge difference.

As basketball legend Michael Jordan once wrote:

> *There is a right way and a wrong way to do things. You can practice shooting eight hours a day, but if your technique is wrong, then all you become is very good at shooting the wrong way.*
>
> *Get the fundamentals down and the level of everything you do will rise.*[xxxiv]

Effective learning is also about developing the very best learning techniques. It constitutes a superior way of controlling and using information.

Abraham Maslow, one of the greatest educational psychologists of the 20th Century, wrote,

> *It is tempting, if the only tool you have is a hammer, to treat every problem as if it were a nail.*[xxxv]

Relying on rote-learning to master huge amounts of content is like using a hammer for every job.

A hammer may be perfect for jobs that require nails, but is of little use if you require screws. And if you have to paint a wall, well...

As well as a strong, positive relationship to learning, the 21st Century student needs to build up an entire tool box of techniques.

The model we have developed to describe the skills and techniques required to train the Learning Mind effectively, is based on decades of working with learners of all levels and ages.

We call it the Hourglass Model and it differs from more traditional models because it stresses:

    i)   Managing information on a 'need to know, want to know' basis;

    ii)   Active understanding, storage and recall of relevant information and concepts;

and

iii)   Synthesis and expression strategies, to create and communicate new understandings and innovations.

The exciting thing about the Hourglass Model is that it works in both innovative learning situations and more traditional learning environments.

This is because the focus is on training students in more advanced and effective learning habits, rather than drilling content.

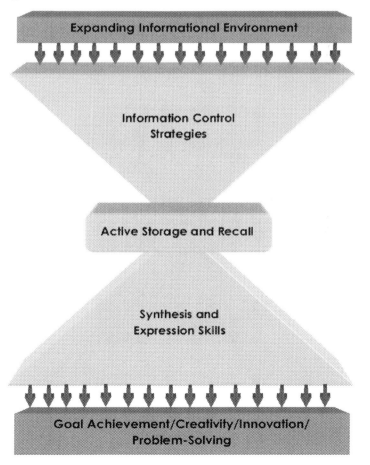

For a student forced to deal with an ever-expanding global learning environment, the first key is to learn to manage the flow of information.

This means developing strategies for identifying and actively understanding the information that is most useful **for the task at hand.**

The 'Chef' Metaphor

Imagine a great chef.

He has been called in to resurrect a struggling restaurant. What is the first thing he must do?

What he **will not do** is rush out to the market and buy up everything in sight. Apart from the unnecessary expense, he would have no way of storing everything.

In an information context, trying to learn 'everything' is self-defeating. The sheer volume, and the fact that most information is not relevant to your needs, will simply lead you down enticing rabbit-holes from which it is sometimes difficult and time-consuming to escape. This is one of the dangers of Facebook or Google – or the on-line world in general – we may end up a very long way from where we were heading when we began.

For this reason, we need a plan...

The Menu

The first thing the chef would do is to decide on a menu – the 20 or so dishes that he will prepare.

The idea is not to offer every dish in the world, but rather to decide on an achievable selection of dishes, and prepare them better than anyone else. That way, people will choose his restaurant over any other.

Using this menu, the chef can prepare a shopping list of the ingredients he actually **needs**. This way there is no wasted effort, time or expense.

Applying this model to learning, we can see the obvious advantage. It is the first step towards managing the chaos of information swirling around us.

For the student in a traditional learning environment, the menu is already there. The syllabus tells us exactly what we are and aren't required to know.

In a less structured environment (like the rest of my life!) the menu is determined by my need at that given moment, whether it be to explore a particular passion or to solve a problem at work.

The Store-Room

Even when our chef has his list of ingredients, he does not immediately go out shopping. If he is organised, he will look in his storeroom to see what ingredients he already has. That way he will know exactly what he still has to acquire.

In learning terms, we call this 'knowing what you don't know'. By organising the task effectively, we can see clearly where our strengths and weaknesses lie – what we already know and what we still need to master. It is a way of focussing our effort and understanding the scope of the work.

Strategies which promote understanding, rather than the memorisation of facts, promote active learning and the formation of concepts. These are both key to storing knowledge that can be synthesised and applied creatively at a later time.

The only truly valuable learning is **transferable** learning. That is, learning that can be used in other contexts, to solve other problems. Naturally, *how* we store information will determine how well we can use it later for future tasks.

Reusable, recyclable knowledge is the essence of creativity.

Making a Meal of It...

The Chef now has his store-room set up. But, of course, simply having the ingredients for a dish does not mean that you can produce a culinary masterpiece. The great chef spends years perfecting the ability to turn raw materials into works of art.

The creative aspect of cooking involves a range of specific skills, which chefs labour hard to master.

In any effective learning plan, this creative aspect of the process should not be under-estimated.

The bottom half of the Hourglass involves the skills of Synthesis and Expression – the creativity and communication skills. In today's world, these skills, too, are a part of any adequate preparation for life.

In the formal education environment, these skills are expressed through traditional forms such as the essay. The modern world however requires a far more comprehensive notion of creativity than the one which presently exists in education systems around the world.

Creativity is a way of thinking that people can be trained to master. In fact, we spend much of our time doing just that.

The principles of creativity are the basis of the third element of the 3-Mind Revolution – the Creative Mind...

Chapter 7

Mind #3: The Creative Mind

A Capacity for Creativity

Creativity has a reputation for being mysterious and unpredictable – a talent that some individuals are just born with, but the truth is that **everybody** is born with a capacity for creativity.

Unfortunately, our natural inclination for forming brain-efficient patterns of behaviour – as essential as it has been in survival terms – has a tendency to significantly limit our creativity as we grow older.

Although the distinction between 'right-brain' and 'left-brain' functions has been drastically overstated for decades, there is enough evidence of left/right lateral differentiation to allow us to still speak, in metaphorical terms, of 'the creative right-brain' and the 'structured and logical left-brain'.

As a broad-stroke, simplified approximation, we can characterise the right-brain as providing a more direct connection with our store of memories and constructs – as the seat of imagination, which associates a new experience or problem with existing patterns and makes connections.

The left-brain can be described as the 'logical' side, controlling processes and structures which we have already mastered, and which can be used to structure our responses to familiar or recognisable stimuli.

From an evolutionary stand-point, this is a great arrangement. The right-brain handles new and perhaps threatening elements, and once something is known and mastered, it passes responsibility over to the left-brain, thus freeing itself up to focus on the next new thing.

In terms of creativity, however, there is one major disadvantage to this arrangement. As the left-brain controls most of the everyday activity, it comes, over time, to dominate the bi-lateral relationship. This is natural, as a vast majority of our everyday lives involve familiar events and tasks. If we had to relearn them every day, we would quickly become overwhelmed.

The effect of this, however, is to 'mindset' us into familiar ways of doing things, and this can create stereotypical behaviour, which hampers our ability to deal with new problems.

In a recent experiment (dubbed the 'Thinking Cap' experiment and featured in media outlets across the world), Professor Snyder demonstrated how the ability to solve a novel problem was significantly increased, if activity in the left fronto-temporal lobe was reduced, using Transcranial Direct-Current Stimulation (tDCS). In the press, this was referred to as 'switching on creativity'[xxxvi].

What it clearly demonstrated, was that the dominance of 'left-brain' processes can negatively affect our ability to think 'outside the box' – that when we become habituated to certain ways of doing things, it can be almost impossible to do things a different way, even if the old way isn't working too well.

Reduce that dominance, even temporarily, and our natural propensity for finding new and different solutions re-asserts itself.

This research is exciting, because it points to the possibility of enhancing human creativity – and not necessarily by designing a portable 'thinking cap' (or rather a 'creativity cap') to temporarily 'turn down' the logic circuits and give the right-brain space to work.

Although such a device is theoretically possible, and may one day exist, the experiment has something more important to say about how we might train the developing brains of the young, unassisted by technology, so that the natural tendency for left-brain dominance isn't further accentuated through bad training.

Given that the brain favours well-practised behaviours over novel ones, this makes it all the more important to avoid anti-creative learning practices like rote-learning and drilling. As Michael Jordan pointed out, if your technique is wrong, then all you become is very good at doing things the wrong way.

If we can create a fun and non-threatening learning environment, then give our children constant experience in the fundamental strategies and habits of creativity, the result will be (to paraphrase 'his Airness') that: 'the level of everything [they] do will rise.'

If the next generation is to be more creative and innovative, then we need to make the habitual behaviours we reinforce through their education as creative and innovative as possible, so that the thought-processes, strategies and mental habits that become their 'first-response' reflex are the more creative ones, best suited to the demanding environment in which they live.

We have made amazing advances, over the past few decades, in our understanding of the human brain, but neuroscientists and psychologists still have a long way to go, before they will be able to unravel exactly how we, as humans, are able to create abstract concepts, especially those which may never previously have existed.

But, understand it or not, creativity is as much a part of our human make-up as anger, joy, love, language or... eye-brows.

Each of us is creative every day.

Every time we think of a solution to a problem; every time we describe something from memory; every time we choose a reply to someone else's question or make a decision, we are exercising our capacity for creativity.

With this in mind, it is comforting to reflect that our role as parents and teachers is a simple one: **to nurture that capacity and do nothing to drive it underground.**

Of course, when people say that this person is highly creative, or that one is not, what they are really doing is making a comparison of creative **outcomes** – judging the idea's **originality** or, perhaps, its **usefulness**.

So, what exactly **is** creativity? And how do we fulfil our role of training the Creative Mind?

The Difference between Imagination and Creativity

Before we discuss what creativity is, we should first discuss what it isn't.

Many people confuse creativity with imagination. However, although they are related, they are not the same thing.

Imagination is, if you like, the non-conscious aspect of the creative process.

It is the brain responding to the environment – and, perhaps, to a problem or a conscious thought-process – by instinctively pulling from the memory loosely-related images, emotions, ideas and other neural patterns, then combining them in random new configurations.

Actually, the Imagination resembles your computer's search engine. Type in a stimulus, and it will automatically pull out of memory anything from your previous experience which in any way remotely connects with the object of the search.

When Lucy asked Linus and Charlie Brown what they thought they saw in the clouds, neither boy's initial responses were conscious.

The brain is a pattern-recognition machine, and in this case, it was operating entirely automatically. It detected vague shapes in the clouds, compared them at lightning speed with its library of stored patterns and began to make matches.

That is imagination. If the stimulus were a question, rather than clouds, then the patterns selected subconsciously might be drawn from more abstract narrative patterns – often in combination.

By the time Linus talks of British Honduras, Thomas Eakin or the apostle Paul, or Charlie Brown suggests a similarity to a duck or a horsey, elements from the non-conscious imagination have already been selected and become conscious. This way, each boy can explain and elaborate on the elements that the Imagination has thrown up.

It might be said that Linus is more creative than his friend. A more accurate description, however, is that he has a more fertile Imagination. This is based, no doubt on a richer experience and, therefore, a more diverse stock of available memories and concepts.

This distinction is important, because although a fertile imagination is a good indicator of potential creativity, the actual quality of an individual's Creative Mind relies on far more.

It has been claimed that:

*'The only proven test for creativity is the creation itself.'*xxxvii

This observation touches on what distinguishes creativity from mere imagination.

Creativity must result in a product.

'Arty-Farty'

Of course, not all creative product is of the same quality.

A creative solution that works for one problem may not work for another. Not all attempts at communicating abstract ideas will be equally effective. One artwork may provide greater aesthetic enjoyment than another – though this is a more subjective judgement.

The success of any creative act must ultimately be judged in relation to the creator's intent. Did it achieve its aim?

A common disclaimer states:

'I don't know Art, but I know what I like.'

In some ways, this statement sums up the difficulty of assessing creative success. Beauty – and, at times, even utility – is in the eye of the beholder. What I think of as a sensational painting might leave you cold – or even disgust you. I may regard as a waste of space a gadget that you find incredibly useful.

Arguments over prize-winners and short-listings in the Arts are testimony to the fact that creativity is notoriously difficult to judge. The more criteria a group of people can agree on, the more likely they are to concur on the quality of a creative product that falls within the scope of those criteria.

The trick, of course, is to get any group of people to agree on anything – especially a rubric for judging Art or Literature!

The difficulty of assessing creative product is one of the key reasons why creativity has been pushed to the periphery of education.

In a system where assessment is king and the primary purpose of education is to 'objectively' rank individual students, evaluation of their creative capacity is often regarded as subjective. It is difficult to fit into a tick-box mentality and so it is eventually consigned to the 'too hard' basket.

Does this mean that we shouldn't judge the products of creative endeavour? Some people think so, but this is short-sighted. After all, if most behaviours have a creative component, then we are judging and evaluating creativity all the time, whether we realise it or not.

Certainly, in the Arts, there is an argument that the artist's vision is unique. One man's installation work is another man's pile of recycled garbage. In some ways, art is the highest expression of human individualism –

which as we have seen, is an essential characteristic of the Champion Mindset. Perhaps the only way to judge art is by how well it achieves the original aim of the artist – and maybe whether that original aim was worth the effort in the first place.

And at what point does individualism become self-indulgence? When does Art become 'Arty-Farty'? If the purpose of art is to communicate the artist's vision, then self-indulgence is counterproductive, because it hampers that communication.

The Creative Purpose

Creativity, unlike the instinctive imagination, has a conscious purpose.

In the post-Pentium world, with its access to a growing array of information technologies, emphasis is on the manipulation and utilization of information, rather than on its accumulation – on what we can do, creatively, rather than what we can store and recall.

Today, more than ever, therefore, creativity needs to focus on its **purpose**. If the purpose of a piece of writing is to communicate, it is useless to claim that the intended readers 'just didn't get it' – as if it were their fault.

If it has failed to communicate, then it has **failed**.

Crafted Imagination

This focus on the end result helps to define the creative process and distinguish it from mere Imagination. To help develop a creative process in any field, from the Arts to industry, we must first be aware of its purpose – of the product we hope to create.

The creative product is a result of what we call 'Crafted Imagination'. How well we craft the output of our Imagination will determine the quality of the final product.

The Creativitree

The diagram below is designed to help explain the relationship between the different elements of creativity.

The metaphor we have chosen is the fruit tree. The roots represent the imagination, the trunk and branches symbolize the structure and the craft, and the leaves and fruit are the creative product.

The Creativitree

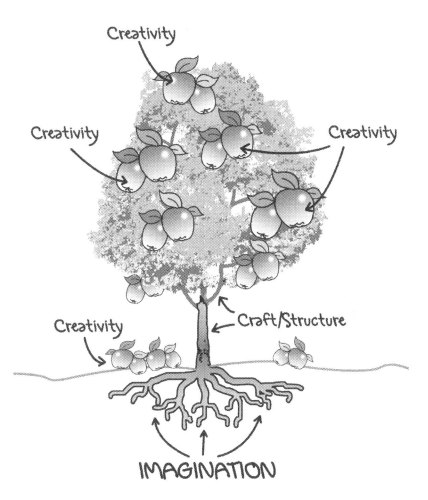

The Roots:

The imagination is the start of the creativity process.

Functioning as the roots of the tree, it draws upon sensory input from the environment and all the knowledge and experiences stored in the fertile soil of the non-conscious mind. As we have seen earlier, this process is sometimes referred to as a 'right-brain' activity, because a significant proportion of the brain activity involved takes place in the right cerebral cortex.

This is why our learning habits, life experiences and education are so important. The more diverse an individual's life experiences, the wider the variety of materials she can draw from.

As we noted earlier, Linus could draw from a wide range of domains, but Charlie Brown's resources were far more limited. This distinction, according to the Snyder research, is one of the classic tests of creative potential.

The good news is that it is never too late to increase our range of interests, and, therefore, our own creative resources.

The Trunk and Branches:

In addition to these raw materials, the tree needs structure in order to grow. This takes the form of a trunk and branches, which nurture and support the leaves, the flowers and then the fruit.

The trunk and branches of the creative process are the craft – the skills and strategies, both conscious and procedural, which can be learned and applied to the ideas thrown up by the imagination.

These skills and strategies order and process the raw materials, conceiving the nature of the finished product – the fruit of the process – 'brain-storming' numerous possible approaches and designing a preferred plan, through which a satisfactory result might be achieved.

This 'left-brain', structured process provides the balance to the uncontrolled flow of imagination, which, unless so structured, will produce little of value, long-term, however it constantly draws upon the 'right-brain' associative qualities to overcome 'road-blocks'. The process is complex and organic and requires the neural coordination of a mental gymnast.

So, rather than being (as is often believed) an entirely mysterious and essentially innate 'gift', creativity, in any area of endeavour, is a 'talent' based on acquired knowledge, defined skills and constant rehearsal.

It is a uniquely human way of thinking that can be pursued, practised – and perfected.

Though the tools and the skills – the craft – of a writer, an artist, a musician, a mathematician, a physicist, an actor, an entrepreneur, a human resources manager, an inventor or a trial lawyer may be very different, all must learn to be creative if they are to be successful.

The common principle shared by all forms of creative activity is the ability to structure imagination to produce a result. And results are the foliage and the fruit of the Creativitree.

Chapter 8

The '3-Mind' Revolution

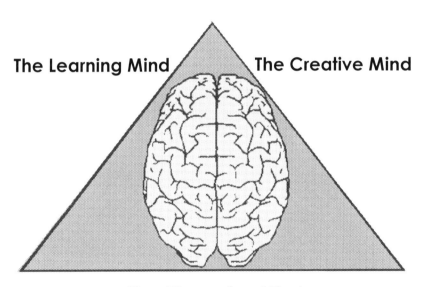

The Learning Mind

The Creative Mind

The Champion Mind

All for One and One for All...

Like the Three Musketeers – or the Holy Trinity – the single human mind is made up of three distinct functions, all working flawlessly together.

The 3-Mind Revolution aims at optimising the relationship between these three minds to nurture the successful 21st Century learner.

If we can train **the Champion Mind** to develop its unique strengths and to recognise the strengths of others, we have a solid foundation upon which to build other skills.

If we can develop **the Learning Mind**, so that we maintain our natural curiosity about the world, and construct, store and use knowledge effectively, we will be able to break through our obsession with detail and focus on *how* we learn.

If we can develop, in **the Creative Mind**, the imagination and the discipline to apply creativity to the problems we face, and if we strive, in our education systems, to give creativity the strong emphasis that it deserves, we can build a world in which everyone has the opportunity and the capability to contribute.

*

Over 400 years ago, Sir Francis Bacon observed that, *'knowledge itself is power.*[xxxviii]

Of course, history has shown that power can be both a blessing and a curse. The world has changed, and we are in the midst of a knowledge explosion. It is up to us to decide whether this change produces a social catastrophe, or an exciting opportunity to overcome the familiar recurrent problems of history.

There is no doubt that future innovations will create even greater prosperity. There is however a real danger of the rich getting richer and the poor getting poorer.

We can already see signs of social and economic polarisation, with a growing gap between the world's haves and have-nots. This 'new feudalism' has the potential to unleash social unrest and ecological disaster.

Luckily, this is not the only possible outcome.

Information technologies can divide or unite us. The choice is ours.

Much will depend on how well we are prepared.

A different but achievable vision of the future stems from the ideal of cooperative creativity: a world of shared productivity and belonging. A world where human innovation means an equitable and sustainable future.

This is a revolutionary vision, and true, universal education is the key to its ultimate success. As parents, teachers and leaders, it is our duty to make this kind of educational experience a reality – for every individual, in every country, on the planet.

Endnotes:

---

i   McLuhan, M., *Understanding Media: The Extensions of Man*, Originally published in 1964 by Mentor, New York; reissued 1994, MIT Press, Cambridge, Massachusetts with an introduction by Lewis Lapham

ii   Sun Tzu, *The Art of War* (China: 4th Century BCE)

iii   The text of this 1993 interview, given when Clarke was 86 years old, shows a visionary who has lived to see many of his ideas come to pass, and who can still look forward to the future. It can be read in full on: http://southasia.oneworld.net/article/view/74591/1?Printable Version=enabled

iv   Attributed to Heraclitus – circa 535 – 475 BCE.

v   Toffler, A., *Powershift: Knowledge, Wealth and Violence at the Edge of the 21st Century* (New York: Bantam Books, 1990).

vi   See Chiem, D. & Caswell, B., *Deeper than the Ocean* (Singapore: Marshall Cavendish Editions, 2007) & *The Art of Communicating with Your Child* (Singapore: Marshall Cavendish Editions, 2008)

vii   Heraclitus (c.535 BCE – 475 BCE), *On the Universe* (Fragment 41).

viii   For a simple, concise look at Gutenberg's historical importance, take a few minutes to visit the website http://intermentary.com/renaissance-computer. It shows the huge influence of the Judeo-Christian emphasis on the importance of the word, and explains the universal uptake of printing across the Western World in the decades following Gutenberg's invention.

ix   It's a fact. Some researchers were actually sadistic enough to try it – though that was at Johns Hopkins University, back in 1882, before modern animal protection laws were enacted. In the experiment the temperature was raised at a rate of 0.002°C. per second, and at the end of 2½ hours the animal was discovered to have died without moving. It was reported by G. Stanley Hall in 1887.

x   The term was coined by Wyndham Lewis in 1948, but popularised by Marshall McLuhan in the early 1960s. In his books *The Gutenberg Galaxy: The Making of Typographic Man* (1962) and *Understanding Media* (1964), McLuhan outlined how the electronic mass media enable people to interact on an unprecedented global scale, exclusive of both time and space. Through this process, the electronic mass media have effectively converted the entire world into a 'village'.

xi   Barth, R., *Learning By Heart*, (San Francisco: Wiley, 2001).

xii   Ramachandran, V.S., *Reith Lectures 2003: The Emerging Mind*. http://www.bbc.co.uk/radio4/reith2003/lecture1.shtml

xiii Ibid.

xiv   Ibid.

xv   Caswell, B. P., Chiem, D. P., & Snyder, A. W., *Narrative Intellect: The Narrative Fractal as the Unifying Principle of Human Intelligence*. (in development at time of publication)

xvi   Ibid.

xvii Miller, G. A., The Magical Number Seven, Plus or Minus Two: Some limits on our capacity for processing information. *Psychological Review*, Vol. 63, No. 2, (1956) pp.81–97.

xviii See, for example:
(1) Shiffrin, R.; Nosofsky, R., Seven plus or minus two: A commentary on capacity limitations, *Psychological Review*, Vol. 101, No. 2, (1994) pp.357–361.
(2) Schweickert, R.; Boruff, B., Short-term memory capacity: Magic number or magic spell? *Journal of Experimental Psychology: Learning, Memory, and Cognition*, Vol. 12, No. 3, (1986) pp. 419–25.
(3) Cowan, N. The magical number 4 in short-term memory: A reconsideration of mental storage capacity. *Behavioral and Brain Sciences*, Vol. 24, No.1, pp.87–114; discussion pp.114–85. (2001).

xix   *Caswell, B.P., Chiem, D.P., Snyder, A.W., op cit*

xx   See:
(1) Snyder A.W. & Mitchell D. J., *Is integer arithmetic fundamental to mental processing? The mind's secret arithmetic*. Proc. R. Soc. Lond. B. Biol. Sci. 266 (1999) pp. 587-92.
(2) Snyder A. W., Paradox of the savant mind, *Nature*, 413 (2001), pp. 251-252.

(3) Snyder, A. W. and Thomas, M., Autistic artists give clues to cognition, *Perception*, 26 (1997) pp. 93-96.

xxi See:

(1) Snyder, A.W., Mulcahy, E., Taylor, J.L., Mitchell, D.J., Sachdev P. and Gandevia S.C.(2003) Savant-like skills exposed in normal people by supressing the left fronto-temporal lobe. *Journal of Integrative Neuroscience*, vol. 2, no. 2, (2003).

(2) Snyder, A.W., Bossomaier, T. and Mitchell, D.J., Concept formation: 'Object' attributes dynamically inhibited from conscious awareness. *Journal of Integrative Neuroscience*, vol. 3, no. 1, (2004) pp. 31-46.

xxii Snyder, A.W., Bossomaier, T. and Mitchell, D.J., Concept formation: 'Object' attributes dynamically inhibited from conscious awareness. *Journal of Integrative Neuroscience*, vol. 3, no. 1, (2004) p. 31.

xxiii (1) Chi, R. P. & Snyder, A. W., Brain stimulation enables the solution of an inherently difficult problem. *Neuroscience Letters*, Vol. 515, No. 2. (2012) pp.121-124.

(2) Gallate, J., Wong, C., Ellwood, S., Chi, R., and Snyder, A., Noninvasive brain stimulation reduces prejudice scores on an implicit association test.
Neuropsychology, vol. 25, no. 2, (2011) pp.185-192.

xxiv Snyder, A., Mitchell, J., Bossomaier, T. & Pallier, G. The creativity quotient: An objective scoring of ideational fluency. *Creativity Research Journal*, Vol. 16, No. 4, (2004) pp.415-420.

xxv Donne, J., *Devotions Upon Emergent Occasions [Meditation XVII]* (England: 1624).

xxvi Barnett, E., Facebook cuts six degrees of separation to four. *Telegraph*, UK. (22 November 2011).

xxvii Titcomb, J., Facebook says there are only 3.57 degrees of separation. *Telegraph*, UK. (4 February, 2016).

xxviii *A Boy Named Charlie Brown*. Director Bill Melendez: U.S.A.(1969)

xxix Snyder, A. W., Chiem, D. P., from a joint speech at the Snyder Theatre, MindChamps Singapore, (2005)

xxx Snyder, A. (ed), *What Makes a Champion!* Melbourne: Penguin, 2002.

xxxi Ibid, p.4

xxxii   Maslow, A.H. (1943). A theory of human motivation. *Psychological Review, Vol.* 50, No. 4, pp.370–396.

xxxiii   See:
         (1) Seligman, M., *Learned Optimism: How to Change Your Mind and Your Life.* (New York: Knopf, 1991).
         (2) Seligman, M., *The Optimistic Child: Proven Program to Safeguard Children from Depression & Build Lifelong Resilience.* (New York: Houghton Mifflin, 1996).
         (3) Seligman, M., *Authentic Happiness: Using the New Positive Psychology to Realize Your Potential for Lasting Fulfillment.* (New York: Free Press, 2002).

xxxiv   Jordan, M., *I Can't Accept Not Trying: Michael Jordan on the Pursuit of Excellence.* (San Francisco: Harper, 1994)

xxxv   Maslow, A., *The Psychology of Science: A Reconnaissance.* (New York: Harper, 1966.)

xxxvi   See:
         (1) Chi, R. P. & Snyder, A. W., Brain stimulation enables the solution of an inherently difficult problem. *Neuroscience Letters,* Vol. 515, No. 2, (2012) pp.121-124.
         (2) Snyder, A. W., Ellwood, S. & Chi R.P., Switching on Creativity. *Scientific American Mind Special Issue.* New York: Scientific American Inc. (Nov/Dec 2012)

xxxvii   Snyder, A., Mitchell, J., Bossomaier, T. and Pallier, G., The creativity quotient: An objective scoring of ideational fluency. *Creativity Research Journal,* Vol.16, No.4, (2004) p.415

xxxviii Bacon, F., *Meditationes Sacrae,* England. (1597)

PRAISE FOR:

Other Bestselling (Non-Fiction) Books by David Chiem and Brian Caswell

DEEPER THAN THE OCEAN

"Deeper than the Ocean is a beautiful fusion of vision-inducing storytelling, juxtaposed with solid scientific evidence... It is a complete 'one-stop' guide for anyone interested in effective learning and development for the children under their care."

Ms Miki Kanamaru, Psychologist, Australia

"Brian Caswell and David Chiem have woven fascinating 'stories' using metaphors and analogies to explain difficult concepts from current neuroscientific research. *Deeper than the Ocean* provides excellent insights and advice for developing a positive self-concept and champion mindset in our children. I recommend this important work enthusiastically to all."

Mrs Carmee Lim, Former Principal of Raffles Girl's Secondary School; Former Executive Director, Principals' Academy; Former Senior Inspector of Schools, Ministry of Education, Singapore

THE ART OF COMMUNICATING WITH YOUR CHILD

"*The Art of Communicating with Your Child* is informative, yet not preaching nor didactic. It is easy to read, but it never insults; it always respects the reader. Finally, it is truthful without being arrogant. In this book, you hold the blueprint for building a Champion for a Lifetime."

Eric Jensen, Internationally-Respected Educator, Author of Enriching the Brain, Co-Founder of Super-Camp

"This is the encyclopaedia parents need to find out why a child is behaving the way he is and how they can learn from a child's communication habits. Appropriate communication approaches are listed in point form together with complete scientific research to back the advice. This book provides easy reading and understanding by explaining theories in a matter-of-fact manner."

Review in Young Parents Magazine, Feb 2009

The creators of cutting-edge learning strategies New Brain Software® and Optimal Flow Method™, Brian Caswell and David Chiem have accumulated between them over 50 years of experience in the domains of education, mind development, film, the literary and performing arts and the creation of active learning programmes for children of all ages.

Brian Caswell: An award-winning author and respected educationist with over 40 years in public and private education, Brian has authored more than 200 books, including novels, short-stories, books for parents and educational professionals. Today, in a technological era, Brian adds electronic reading and phonics books to his repertoire of authored books. Brian is the MindChamps® Dean of Research and Program Development.

David Chiem: With a distinguished background in film, television and the theatre, David is widely recognised as a Master-trainer in the field of advanced learning strategies and in the application of dramatic techniques to learning. He is Founder, Chairman and Group CEO of MindChamps®. David has crossed many bridges of success to achieve a remarkable synthesis of art, education and entrepreneurship.

Brian and David have previously co-authored *Only the Heart* **and** *The Full Story* **– two novels, as well as a series of parenting books including the critically-acclaimed** *Deeper than the Ocean, Art of Communicating with Your Child* **and** *Talking with the Sky*.

Brian and David have taught, trained and lectured to over 350,000 people internationally on advanced learning strategies, parenting, literature and creativity.

The illustrations in this book are by Malcolm McGookin.

Printed in the United States
By Bookmasters